Dealing Crack

The Northeastern Series in Criminal Behavior
edited by GIL GEIS

Armed Robbers in Action
Richard T. Wright & Scott H. Decker

Burglars on the Job
Richard T. Wright & Scott H. Decker

Dealing
CRACK

The Social World of Streetcorner Selling

BRUCE A. JACOBS

foreword by James F. Short Jr.

NORTHEASTERN
UNIVERSITY PRESS
BOSTON

NORTHEASTERN UNIVERSITY PRESS
Copyright 1999 by Bruce A. Jacobs

Library of Congress Cataloging-in-Publication Data

Jacobs, Bruce, 1945–
    Dealing crack : the social world of streetcorner selling / Bruce A. Jacobs : foreword by James F. Short, Jr.
        p. cm. — (The Northeastern series in criminal behavior)
    Includes bibliographical references and index.
        ISBN 1-55553-388-4 (cloth : alk. paper). — ISBN 1-55553-387-6 (paper : alk. paper)
        1. Drug abuse—United States.   2. Narcotics dealers—United States.   3. Crack (Drug)—United States.   4. Cocaine habit—United States.   I. Title.   II. Series.
    HV5825.J3   1999
    364.1′77′0973—dc21   98-45390

Designed by Christopher Kuntze
Composed in Aldus by G&S Typesetters, Inc., in Austin, Texas. Printed and bound by Thomson-Shore, Inc., in Dexter, Michigan. The paper is Glatfelter Supple Opaque Recycled, an acid-free sheet.

MANUFACTURED IN THE UNITED STATES OF AMERICA
03 02 01 00 99   5 4 3 2 1

CONTENTS

FOREWORD
On Experiences Shared and Lessons Learned

My personal forays in ethnography have been few. Those experiences, however, long ago convinced me of how demanding fieldwork is—in energy, honesty, intelligence, and subtlety. Beyond this, I have come to appreciate the importance of the reported experiences and insights imparted by many fieldworkers and informants (graduate student observers, urban ethnographers, anthropologists, and "detached workers" —in my case, young men assigned to work with street gangs in Chicago). In this book Bruce Jacobs reinforces my appreciation for the demands of fieldwork and for what it can tell us. Permit me a brief personal example.

Nearly forty years ago, in the early stages of the Chicago gang project with which I was associated for many years, a graduate student reported on an evening's observation in a pool hall hangout of a gang we were studying and alerted us to the importance of intimate, detailed knowledge of observed places and activities. The pool hall was a place where young and old met and socialized but where outsiders, unless they were regulars or legitimized by them, were unwelcome. In the course of the evening the gang's detached worker asked the graduate student if he was aware of the drug traffic in the pool hall. He was not, though it was happening literally in front of his eyes. He had noted that an attractive girl occasionally took the pool cue from one of the gang members, but the young man's behavior appeared little different from that of others in the group. In fact, his behavior was quite different, for he alone among the gang members was selling heroin (he was also the only hard-drug user in the gang, though many of the others smoked marijuana). The girl was a prostitute who sold drugs, leaving the more dangerous aspects of the task (carrying and delivering heroin) to the gang member, who did not know who was buying his heroin. The girl made the necessary contacts with customers and collected the money, she relieved the gang member of his pool cue, the gang member placed the drug in the pocket of a coat that was hung casually on the wall, and the customer could realize his purchase from the coat pocket.

The point is not so much that our graduate student's observations would have been inaccurate had he not been aware of this activity but that they would have been incomplete without the detached worker's knowledge and sophistication.

In this book, Jacobs takes us through the history of crack manufacture, use, and distribution—its rise and its decline, the plight and the motivation of crack dealers, and the vicissitudes of their existence. It is not a pretty story. Street crack dealers are at the bottom of the system of cocaine production and distribution and are the most vulnerable to ripoffs by other dealers, customers, and anyone else who sees them as a possible source of easy money. They are the most vulnerable to arrest and harassment by police. They also are the most poorly equipped to earn a living legitimately, though many try time and again. Improved economic conditions, in fact, have helped many to get out of dealing.

Jacobs reminds us that there are no hard and fast rules about how to succeed in fieldwork and that it is difficult to be alone and on your own in the field. The work often demands quick decisions, flexibility, high intelligence, and guts. Budding fieldworkers will do well to read his account of his encounters with police and the importance of these encounters for validating his presence in the field.

As Jacobs notes—and as has been well documented by others—the crack cocaine epidemic was of relatively short duration and was limited to the largely African American underclass living in heavily populated inner-city areas. Although customers frequently came from other groups and other areas of cities, crack usage was never widespread beyond those boundaries.

The natural history of crack cocaine is intriguing and instructive. Its spread and organization conformed to none of the theories that might have applied—organization or collective behavior, youth culture or delinquent behavior. Yet the impact of crack on the truly disadvantaged and their communities was profound.

The story of how and why crack fell out of favor is also instructive. Crack never became cool among middle-class youth, and the fearsome effects of heavy usage and addiction contributed to its rejection as the drug of choice among all but a relatively few. Crack usage declined as it became stigmatized. There are lessons here for the control of other drugs, though Jacobs warns of the likelihood of the return to favor of heroin and other drugs. A fundamental truth seems apparent, however. Preferences in such matters are elastic, and control of demand is more likely to succeed than are efforts directed toward supply.

James F. Short Jr.

ACKNOWLEDGMENTS

Any sociologist will tell you that reality is socially constructed. This usually is taken to mean that reality is what people agree that it is. But reality is built in a more literal sense, through the efforts of individuals working together to understand the world around them. Nowhere is this demonstrated more clearly than in the writing of an academic book, where intellectual sparring between author and critic is the rule rather than the exception. I would like to take this opportunity to thank some of my able sparring partners.

A number of them are persons with whom I have never made direct contact. Their intellectual influence, however, has been undeniable. The work of Elijah Anderson, Philippe Bourgois, Eloise Dunlap, Erving Goffman, John Hagan, Laud Humphreys, Bruce Johnson, John Laub, Karl Marx, Bill McCarthy, Robert Prus, Robert Sampson, Georg Simmel, and Glenn Walters has been incontestably important in the development of this book.

In a more immediate sense, I would like to thank Bob Bursik, Janet Lauritsen, and Rick Rosenfeld for their helpful working comments—particularly on chapters 3 and 7. Bob's take on the social organization of "drug sails" is rivaled only by his choice of food and attire. Here's to the underground, Bob. Thanks also go to Scott Decker for providing the resources and working environment necessary to complete a study of this nature. Scott's departmental leadership is greatly appreciated.

Many, many thanks go to Jim Short for his close reading of the book, incisive comments, and thoughtful foreword. Rarely have I encountered an academic of Professor Short's intellectual stature who is as gracious, supporting, and generous. I also would like to express my gratitude to Gil Geis, whose editorial suggestions and insights streamlined the book as only he can, and to Bill Frohlich, who as director of Northeastern University Press provided useful editorial comments while shepherding the book the whole way.

Extra special thanks go to Richard Wright, without whose help this book would not have been possible. Richard put me into contact with Jeff Ferrell to write a chapter for an edited methods anthology published by Northeastern University Press. Scott Brassart, then editor at Northeastern, read the chapter, liked it, and asked if I would like to write a book-length monograph. Beyond his networking assistance, Richard read every word of every chapter, providing suggestions, turns of phrases, and alternative interpretations whenever the situation called for it. Other young academics should be as lucky to receive the mentoring provided by Professor Wright. The path from his office to mine is well worn, a testament to his unceasing efforts to make this monograph as readable and substantively rich as possible. That he was able to time his efforts around excursions to the gym testifies to his powers of organization, if nothing else—as anyone who has seen the inside of his office will tell you.

Thanks go to my parents, Frank and Lynn Jacobs, for bringing me into this world, for instilling in me the importance of the intellectual tradition, and for providing the support and resources to pursue it. Jennifer Johnson, finally, deserves a very special concluding mention. As Bob Bursik once told me, it takes a uniquely devoted person to be willing to marry an academic. JJ is indeed such an individual. Her patience, caring, understanding, and support have been invaluable, in good times and in bad.

The research on which this book is based was funded by Grant No. S-3-40453 from the University of Missouri Research Board. The points of view or opinions expressed are those of the author and do not necessarily represent those of the UMRB.

Portions of chapters 5 and 6 were reprinted with permission from *Justice Quarterly* (The Academy of Criminal Justice Sciences) 13 (1996): 359–81 and *Criminology* 34 (1996): 409–31, respectively.

Dealing Crack

1 Researching Crack

The first public mention of crack cocaine appeared unceremoniously in 1985, buried in a *New York Times* article on drug treatment.[1] Named for its characteristic crackling sound when heated and smoked, crack transfixed Americans in unprecedented numbers as reports of the drug's "instant addictiveness"—and the lengths to which users would go to get more of it—began to flood the media. The CBS News program *48 Hours on Crack Street* reached 15 million viewers, becoming one of the most watched documentaries in the history of television. With *Cocaine Country*, NBC News finished a six-month stretch in which the network broadcast over 400 reports about the drug. Joining the media circus, President Bush during a nationally televised address in fall 1989 positioned a large plastic bag of crack on the desk of the Oval Office, a cache allegedly purchased by undercover agents across the street from the White House in Lafayette Park. America was in a drug panic, and crack was its centerpiece.[2]

Academic research was slow to catch up with the furor. Scientific data concerning the use, abuse, and sale of crack were virtually absent until 1990—fully five years after the drug's appearance on the street scene. The sluggish pace of federal funding at the time critically delayed research regarding the epidemic, and this, in turn, delayed the development of policies to thwart, or at least slow, the burgeoning plague.[3] Re-

3

search has since caught up. Hundreds of articles and dozens of important monographs on crack use and distribution have been published. With all the attention paid to crack in the past decade, one may justifiably wonder whether there is anything left to learn. There is a great deal.

Crack cocaine is produced by cooking cocaine hydrochloride with baking soda to convert the hydrochloride salt into base form. It is among the most successful and recent of drug innovations. The process is technically simple and relatively quick and requires few tools or laboratory supplies. Crack is called the fast-food version of powder cocaine: individual doses are accessible to all but the poorest of the poor, delivering within five seconds a "penetrating euphoria" that has been likened to an all-over body orgasm.[4] The drug's "pharmacological omnipotence"—part myth, part reality—is said to dwarf the high produced by any other currently available illicit drug. Some have suggested that the euphoragenicity (that is, the euphoric kick or rush) of crack is unmatched by any other substance. Unlike other drugs, such as heroin or marijuana, crack cocaine seems to provide no satiation point. It is rare for users to have a single hit, and addicts often say they can never really ingest enough of it. Compulsive, binge-type use is common and ceases only when the user's resources or physical ability are exhausted. As one crack user put it, "It's like a Ruffle potato chip. You can't have just one. Once you take the first blast, then the whole night is going to be an adventure into madness."[5]

In rock form, cocaine can be sold on the streets for five times its wholesale price, depending on the size of the rock. This factor unleashed "the energy of thousands of wanna-be mom-and-pop entrepreneurs who were only too eager to establish high-profit, high-risk retail crack businesses."[6] Crack rapidly expanded the opportunity structure for street-level drug selling. Entrepreneurs facilitated access to supplies, offered controlled selling territories, and created entry-level roles in drug selling that required only minimal training and start-up capital. By 1988, crack was the most widely sold and most profitable substance in the street drug market. Open crack cocaine dealing on city streets from New York to Los Angeles quickly became a fact of urban life. It was a mass-marketing craze that "would have made McDonald's proud." A criminal underground system of distribution and profiteering, unrivaled in the modern era, developed to go with it.[7]

In St. Louis and other metropolitan areas, urban drug markets came to be controlled by self-employed, freelance sellers—some gang affiliated, others not. Intense competition and turf wars soon defined the scene as the urban drug landscape experienced rapid deregulation and destabilization. Epidemic levels of homicides and assaults resulted, not surprising given the drug's pharmacology, fights over territorial boundaries, and sellers bent on propagating a fearsome "don't mess with me" reputation. Community institutions were woefully unprepared for the crisis. Social controls, both formal and informal, broke down. Coupled with a high level of residential mobility and loss of economic opportunity, the wholesale destruction of communities and individuals took on a life of its own. Once peaceful neighborhoods were transformed into urban badlands that persons traversed at their own peril.[8]

As early as 1990, however, the epidemic began to show evidence of remission as new users failed to replace old ones at the rate old users quit. Quantitative indicators have since documented meaningful and significant reductions in rates of crack consumption in major cities across the country over the past ten years. Nationwide, powerful anticrack conduct norms have arisen in response to the personal and social devastation the drug has wrought. To be labeled a crackhead is to be considered the "lowest of the low" in the hierarchy of the streets. Reliance on street crack is typical of persons who have reached advanced stages of dependence and is seen as an act of desperation and foolishness. Youths are known to ridicule and beat up such persons as a pastime, claiming they are nuisances, thieves, and disgraces to the neighborhood. Perhaps in response, ostracized users are resorting to the drug in more innocuous, less stigmatizing ways. Thus, small nuggets of crack are being rolled into marijuana cigarettes and smoked (called *chewy blunts* or *primos* on the streets). This method tempers the drug's effects, mitigates the binge-use cycle that characterizes crack consumption, and tends to obscure the fact that one is indeed still using crack. It is safe to say that as of mid-1998, crack use, with a few rare exceptions in smaller midwestern locales, is in either nationwide decline or (late) plateau. Rates of positive urinalysis for cocaine do remain high in some areas, but significant drops in the number of young users—those at highest risk for becoming chronic adult users—recently have been demonstrated, and this trend is expected to continue.[9]

Active, street-level crack markets are saturated and increasingly unprofitable. Inner-city youths are becoming reluctant to sell crack and are faring relatively poorly if they decide to do so. Many have learned that early and rapid success is unlikely. Some crack sellers have added or shifted to heroin—or report wanting to if conditions become right. Some researchers have found that those who sold only crack in the late 1980s now are selling crack, heroin, or cocaine powder or all three simultaneously.[10]

Given the unfavorable supply and demand dynamics that characterize street crack markets around the country, one wonders why curbside sellers persist at all. By and large, they serve a small set of compulsive smokers responsible for more than 70 percent of all cocaine consumption. As already noted, their numbers are dwindling, as is the amount of money such persons have available for purchases.[11] Recent changes in public transfer payments (such as welfare, AFDC, disability, and social security) only magnify this effect. The fact that vendors sell in a high-risk, legally sanctioned context replete with predators, including the very people they sell with and to, makes the prospect of dealing even less attractive. That these sellers have not disappeared from the streetcorner landscape underscores their desperation or perhaps an inability more than an unwillingness to escape the street scene. Exploring the form and content of their persistence is a central purpose of this book.

Studies of drugs and drug markets in decline are scarce. As Johnson et al. note, "drug era 'declines' and/or 'persistence' have rarely been studied or made a focus for analytic research and have not been well conceptualized by policy makers."[12] Researchers tend to study drugs and drug epidemics as they incubate and expand. At these times, the topic is sexiest and—more important—most fundable. Perhaps there also is a perception that everything is already known; once important issues no longer seem as meaningful or significant. This is a mistake. We have something to learn from those who persist in the face of conditions that tell them they should not.

Though this book explores crack selling in a context of stagnation, it acknowledges that the decline of one drug often signals the rise of another. The book seeks to provide insights into processes that precede important career shifts in drug-use and drug-selling activity.[13] Qualitative research of the kind presented here indicates emergent phenomena and provides information on changing street-level drug markets before official data become available. The book takes a naturalistic approach—presenting issues from the perspective of the actors involved.[14] It asks readers to think of crack dealing as a flow of illicit activity, bounded by constraints of law enforcement and potential criminal victimization and yet imbued with freewheeling entrepreneurism and expressive action. The book, finally, explores crack selling as an interconnected social system of activity. The basis for this approach is the notion that complex and intricate relationships among parts of an organism cannot be explored out of the context of their whole. The focus, therefore, takes a "processual conception of reality," examining how subparts of assorted topics fit into a "meaningful and integrated whole."[15]

Previous research on crack selling, by contrast, tends to present issues singly and myopically. The "critical impact of competition" on motivation and drug market organization, for example, "is almost never mentioned in published [research] because competition is never conceptualized."[16] Competition in the world of crack cocaine sales and use, in both implicit and explicit ways, is a primary concern of the present book. Competition guides individual behavior, catalyzes forms of collective action, shapes methods of transactional security, and mediates career trajectories. The paradoxes that result—between accessibility and secrecy, vulnerability and insulation, risk and security, agency and structure—take on an intrinsic importance and a generic significance for settings beyond the world of street crack.

SETTING AND RESPONDENTS

Like other post–World War II Rustbelt cities of its general size and type, St. Louis has suffered rapid deindustrialization, population loss, resource deprivation, and urban decay. Mobility to surrounding suburbs is high and continues unabated, taking important tax revenue and social capital with it. Since 1990, St. Louis has lost 15 percent of its population; 9,000 residents left in 1997 alone. The city's base of 341,000 makes the impact of such trends acute. St. Louis is developing a concentrated population of the truly disadvantaged—people with scarce resources and abundant social service needs that cannot be met and are getting worse. Such conditions provide an ideal context for drug use, drug selling, and other serious criminality.[17]

St. Louis's crime rate consistently exceeds that of most U.S. urban locales. In 1993, the city's homicide and robbery rates were third highest in the nation, and the rate of serious assault was second. In 1995, the St. Louis violent crime index was 3,356 per 100,000, nearly five times higher than the national rate. The St. Louis homicide rate, at fifty-four per 100,000, was among the highest of any American city and nearly six times higher than the national rate. Increases and decreases in these rates—though at a different scale—tend to mirror other U.S. cities. This makes St. Louis an ideal laboratory for investigating important correlates of crime such as drug selling.[18]

Historically, St. Louis has had one of the largest illicit drug markets in the midwestern United States. In many neighborhoods, crack, heroin, marijuana, and PCP are sold openly and are available throughout the day—particularly on the troubled north side, where social disorganization and urban decay are most pronounced. St. Louis arrestees persistently have high rates of cocaine-, opiate-, and marijuana-positive urine specimens; they are among the highest of the twenty-four cities measured in the Drug Use Forecasting program. Emergency room cases involving cocaine and heroin mirror other large metropolitan areas and indicate a high degree of street drug institutionalization. Though street gangs neither control nor direct drug sales in St. Louis, the nearly 1,500 members of forty-five different gangs facilitate them by providing the microstructural networks and mass of contacts necessary for the trade to thrive.[19]

Among the most socially distressed and impoverished areas in the St. Louis metropolitan area, the study neighborhood generally outranks other local sectors in the percentage of people living at or below poverty, proportions of citizens unemployed or on welfare, dropout rates of children of school age, drug arrests, substance abuse rates, and various indicators of poor health. The study neighborhood and contiguous blocks have all the earmarks of an "urban dead zone"—abandoned buildings, burned-out tenements, garbage-strewn vacant lots, and graffiti-splashed walls. Groups of young men collect on the street, selling crack, "insulting one another's sexual prowess, getting high, and looking for an opportunity to make some fast cash."[20]

The extent to which any given drug market has matured is said to be a function of the quantity of sales and range of hours that drugs are available to sell.[21] The greater the number of hours a market is open, for example, the more developed it tends to be. By these indicators, the market in which this study takes place is a schizophrenic one of sorts, a market in which users can purchase at virtually any hour but where retail units tend to be small, where sellers are disorganized and often predatory, and where overall sales frequencies vary widely depending on the time of day, the day of the week, or the week of the month. The study setting may be characterized generally as active but stagnating. Sales volume is in chronic stagnation, as competition from nearby sellers within and without the dealing set diffuses sales and dilutes profits.

The study population is made up of curbside (streetcorner) distributors, consisting of persons who "routinely sell crack in the same area, [though] each is a freelancer with his own supplier and responsible for his own profits and losses."[22] Similar to Waldorf's 1993 San Francisco sample, these sellers are gang affiliated but not gang directed. This book, therefore, is not about street gang members who sell crack but about crack sellers who happen to be street gang members. Though the public widely perceives gangs to drive street drug selling, research has consistently demonstrated the rarity of such a phenomenon. Inner-city street gangs do not have exclusive control over crack distribution, and many street distributors are not gang members. Gang membership and crack selling correlate but in a facilitating way: gangs provide the connections and criminal capital necessary to do business. Street gangs, however, are unable to develop and implement hierarchical, functionally interdependent structures that would allow a formal business of selling to happen.[23]

As freelancers, the offenders in my sample are rarely fronted supplies (given crack to sell and allowed to pay for it later), sell for their own individual profit, and generally are in constant competition for a small number of compulsively addicted daily smokers who always try to negotiate the price down. Not infrequently, a number of sellers work the same street, corner, or vacant lot at the same time. Though not always blatant or obtrusive, transactions may easily be observed if looked for. Any organization between or among sellers tends to be crude, primitive, and fleeting. House sales are uncommon because the offenders usually lack access to private dwellings in which to do business. Their "collective orientation" as street gang members also is far too weak to support a social organization conducive to selling from private dwellings.[24] Though Fleisher notes that gang-affiliated, street-level crack sellers often pay crack-addicted welfare mothers "rent" (in the form of crack) to use their apartments as dope houses,[25] I did not observe this behavior here (though it probably occurred on occasion).

ETHNOGRAPHY AND ACTIVE OFFENDERS

Though some dismiss ethnography as "the poor sociologist's substitute for the novel,"[26] the importance of qualitative methods for the study of deviant populations cannot be over-stated. Qualitative methods provide a thoroughgoing exploration of the daily behaviors and careers of often hidden or hard-to-reach populations. Such methods allow researchers to decode the manner in which these persons and groups communicate and to describe a body of knowledge or cognition not easily understood by outsiders. Street ethnographies of illicit drug dealers document and explain a wide range of inter-related attitudes, conduct norms, and interaction patterns.[27]

Yet studying active drug dealers is difficult and challenging precisely because their activity is criminal. Active offenders are generally "hard to locate because they find it necessary to lead clandestine lives. Once located, they are reluctant, for similar reasons, to give accurate and truthful information about themselves."[28] By definition, criminological fieldworkers seek to explore the lives of those engaged in felonies where exposure could mean hard prison time. Outside observers represent a potential legal threat, a fact that impedes a good deal of ethnographic work. The more illegal the behavior, the more offenders have to lose if found out. Individuals may refuse to cooperate or may give less than reliable answers to protect their privacy. It is no surprise that outsiders—such as researchers—are often perceived as narcotics officers seeking to obtain damaging evidence for juridical purposes.[29] Indeed, the most common suspicion that subjects have about fieldworkers is that they are spies of some sort. As Sluka notes, "It is difficult to find an [ethnographer] who has done fieldwork who has not encountered this suspicion." [30] In street drug markets, the "basic cultural rule is to treat everyone as a snitch or the man [police] until proven otherwise." [31]

Collecting data from drug dealers, particularly active ones, is likely to be difficult and dangerous unless one can construct friendships within a dealing community. Because this is arduous and sometimes dangerous, some researchers work in institutional settings. Such settings afford the chance to obtain data without the risk of physical harm associated with street interviews. Unfortunately, collecting accurate data in such settings may not be possible; criminologists have "long suspected that offenders do not behave naturally" in criminal justice settings.[32] As Sutherland and Cressey note, "Those who have had intimate contacts with criminals 'in the open' know that criminals are not 'natural' in police stations, courts, and prisons and that they must be studied in their everyday life outside of institutions if they are to be understood." [33] Polsky is more emphatic, insisting that

We can no longer afford the convenient fiction that in studying criminals in their natural habitat, we . . . discover nothing really important that [cannot] be discovered from criminals behind bars. What is true for studying the gorilla of zoology is likely to be even truer for studying the gorilla of criminology.[34]

There also are fundamental differences between the two types of offenders. Institutionalized drug dealers more often may represent those not sophisticated or skilled enough to prevent apprehension or those who do not care about getting caught and sell to anyone, as long as they have money. The failure to account for these differences is "the most central bogeyman in the criminologist's demonology." [35]

HIDDEN POPULATIONS AND METHODOLOGICAL ENTRY

Streetcorner crack dealers are one of many hidden populations. Some researchers view this notion in terms of a group's reachability, referring to its size relative to the broader population, the ease or difficulty in selecting members to interview, and the extent to which reliable responses can be obtained. A more useful characterization, however, would refer first to a group's low social visibility. This is a function of the stigmatized or illegal behaviors its members engage in and actively conceal (or attempt to) from outsiders. Streetcorner crack sellers are therefore a paradox, of sorts: there is perhaps no other openly observable and publicly accessible behavior as negatively sanctioned by law as streetcorner crack selling. It must be so for dealers to be available to their customers.[36]

Knowing this, I began frequenting a neighborhood known for open street-level crack sales. The area is marked by racial and ethnic diversity so it is easy for most anyone to blend in. Over a nine-month span in 1994 to 1995, I made myself familiar to the regular crowd. Some of these persons spent entire days in the district smoking, drinking, playing music, and begging. Though not crack dealers themselves, they knew who the dealers were and where they worked. I was shown these congregation spots.

For weeks, I would either walk or slowly drive through the area to try to be recognized, attempting to capitalize on what Goffman has called second seeings: "under some circumstances if he and they see each other seeing each other, they can use this fact as an excuse for an acquaintanceship greeting upon next seeing."[37] Unfortunately, this process did not go as easily as Goffman suggests. When I drove by, crack dealers yelled "SCAT" at me, screams accentuated with derisive looks and obscene gestures. SCAT is an acronym for "street-corner apprehension team." This fifteen-man undercover team is charged with curbing street-level drug sales by apprehending dealers immediately after sales to one of their "buy" officers. Hiding nearby in unmarked cars, personnel swoop down on offenders in an attempt to catch them with the marked money just given to them by purchasing officers. This money has either traceable dye or serial numbers previously recorded that link dealers to undercover transactions. SCAT units were both feared and loathed, being reportedly merciless in their arrest procedures, which involved strip searches and no breaks.

A few more weeks passed and more trips, but I had yet to make any direct contact. Finally, I decided to get out of my car and approach the individuals I had seen dealing. Though this classic ethnographic technique of approaching strangers and initiating dialogue is said to be ineffective with drug dealers,[38] I tried anyway. I told the dealers who I was and that I wished to take a few minutes out of their day to interview them about street life. Predictably they scoffed, accused me of being "the poh-lice," and instructed me to "get the hell out of here." Two days later, I tried again. I showed the dealers my university identification and told them that the interviews would be confidential and anonymous and that they would be paid for their time and effort. It was the money that was critical in generating their interest—even the modest sum that I offered. On the streets, money talks; nobody does anything for nothing.

Though I had made contact, making that contact stick proved difficult because dealers still suspected that I was tied to law enforcement in some way. Ironically, the police gave me my biggest credibility boost.

POLICE AND CREDIBILITY

Ferrell notes that "a researcher's strict conformity to legal codes can be reconceptualized as less a sign of professional success than a possible portent of methodological failure. A willingness to break the law," by contrast, "[opens] up a variety of methodological possibilities"[39]—and dangers as well. Breaking the law puts the researcher at risk for trouble with the police and with the organization that employs him or her.

Hanging out with offenders on street corners, driving them around in my car, and visiting their homes must have been a curious sight. My appearance is somewhat like that of a college student. Shorts, t-shirts, casual boots, and baseball caps with rounded brims—"just like SCAT wear them," as one dealer put it—are my typical attire. Further, I am white, clean-cut, and affect a middle-class appearance—traits the relatively poor, African American respondents associate with the police.

To offenders who hadn't gotten to know me well or were waiting to pass judgment, I was seen as being on a deep-cover assignment designed to unearth their secrets and put them in jail. To cops on the beat, I was just another college boy driving down to crackville with a user in tow to buy for him. Such relations are commonplace in the street-level drug scene and have generalized subcultural currency: users serve as middlemen and funnel unfamiliar customers to dealers for a finder's fee, usually in drugs and without the customer's consent (for being "taxed," that is) but generally with his or her tacit permission. When cops see a nicely dressed, clean-shaven white boy, wearing a baseball cap, with a black street person in the passenger seat of a late-model car (a car with out-of-state plates, I might add), they scent that business is in the offing.

Several police stops of me in a one-month period lent some credibility to this. I had not obtained, as other researchers studying active offenders had, a "prior agreement with the police" whereby they knew what I was doing and pledged not to interfere.[40] I chose not to. The last thing I wanted was to let police know what I was doing. As Polsky explains,

Most of the danger for the fieldworker comes not from the cannibals and headhunters but from the colonial officials. The criminologist studying uncaught criminals in the open finds sooner or later that law enforcers try to put him on the spot—because, unless he is a complete fool, he uncovers information that law enforcers would like to know.[41]

Because my grant was not federally funded, I could not protect the identity of my respondents with a certificate of confidentiality (which theoretically bars police from obtaining data that pertain to one's subjects). My work was undercover in a sense and eminently discreditable. But contrary to admonitions by some to avoid contact with the police while doing research with dangerous populations,[42] my run-ins with police turned out to be the most essential tool for establishing my credibility.

My first run-in came two weeks after making initial contact with offenders. I was driving a field contact (an active crack seller) through a crack-filled neighborhood—a neighborhood that also happened to have the highest murder rate in a city with the fourth-highest murder rate in the nation. We were approaching a group of ten midteen youths and were about to stop when a St. Louis City patrol car pulled behind. Should I stop, as I planned on doing, get out, and talk with these youth (some of whom the field contact marginally knew), or would that place them in imminent danger of arrest? Or should I continue on as if nothing was really going on, even though I had been driving stop and go, under ten miles an hour, prior to and during the now slow-speed pursuit? I opted for the latter, accelerating slowly in a vain attempt to reassert a "normal appearance."[43]

Sirens went on. I pulled over and reassured my field contact there was nothing to worry about since neither of us had contraband (I hoped). As officers approached, I thought about what to tell them. Should I say I was a university professor doing field research on crack dealers (a part I clearly didn't look), lie, or say nothing at all? "What you doin' down here?" one of the officers snapped. "Exit the vehicle, intertwine your fingers behind your heads, and kneel with your ankles crossed," he commanded. The searing June sidewalk was not conducive to clear thinking, but I rattled something off. "We used to work together at ——. I waited tables, he bussed, and we been friends since. I'm a sociology major up at —— and he said he'd show me around the neighborhood sometime. Here I am." "Yeah right," the cop snapped again while searching for the crack he thought we already had purchased. Three other police cars arrived, as the cop baited my field contact and me as to how we really knew each other, what each other's real names were (which neither of us knew at the time), and what we were doing here. Dissatisfied with my answers, a sergeant took over, lecturing me on the evils of crack and how it would destroy a life others in this very neighborhood wished they had. I found no fault with the argument, listened attentively, and said nothing. After a final strip search in the late afternoon sun revealed nothing, they let us go, said I was lucky, and vowed to take me in if I ever showed my face again.

On a second occasion, my field contact and one of his crack-selling friends were in my car when we pulled up to a local liquor store. The two offenders became nervous on seeing two suits in a "tec" (detective) car parked at the phone booth. I told the two to wait while I went into the store. As I exited, the two men approached me and showed their badges. "What you doin' with these guys? Do you know 'em?" "Yes," I said, deciding to tell them who I *really* was and what I was doing. "Mind if we search your car?" one asked. "No problem," I replied. "Go right ahead." As one searched my car (for crack, guns, or whatever else he thought he'd find), his partner cuffed both of the offenders and ran warrants. As I soon learned, both detectives knew the two as repeat violent offenders with long rap sheets. "I respect what you're doing," the searching officer said as he finished and approached, "but you don't know who you're dealing with. These guys are no good." I told him thanks and promptly left.

On a third occasion, I was sitting on my car making small talk with four or five dealers, when a patrol car rolled by. The officers inside gave a stern look and told us to break it up. "Alright," I said, not going anywhere. We continued to talk for a few minutes when the officers, clearly agitated, rolled by again and demanded in no uncertain terms, "Break it up, and we mean now." I hopped in my car, drove four or five blocks, made a left and heard sirens. "Here we go again." This time, I was not nearly as nervous as on the other occasions, ready to dispense my professor line, show my consent forms and faculty ID, and see their shocked reaction. "Get out of the car and put your hands on the trunk," the driver predictably ordered as I began my explanation. They searched me anyway, perhaps thinking it was just another mendacious story, but I kept conversing in a relaxed, erudite tone. Cops are known to have perceptual shorthands to render quick and accurate typifications of those with whom they're interacting,[44] and I could tell my conversational style was creating a good impression. I told them I was doing interviews, that I was paying respondents for their time, and that the research was part of a university grant designed to better understand the everyday lives of urban youth. This was of course specious. The study's true purpose was to explore crack selling, something I dared not admit for obvious reasons. "You can do what you want," one of them said, satisfied after a thorough search revealed no contraband, "but if I were you, I'd be real careful. You don't want to mess around with these punks."

I did not realize it at the time, but these episodes with the police were absolutely essential to my research. Police provided the test I desperately needed to pass if my study were to be successful. The differential enforcement practices of these officers—where young minority males are singled out as the "symbolic assailants" and "suspicious characters" deserving of attention[45]—benefited me immensely. Police detained me because I was with them. Driving alone in these same areas at the same time—though suspicious—would not likely have attracted nearly as much attention. I was "guilty by association" and "deserving" of the scrutiny young black males in many urban locales receive consistently. For my research, at least, this differential enforcement was anything but negative.

As Douglas notes, it is often necessary to convince offenders that a researcher does not represent or work for the authorities.[46] Sluka adds that subjects "are going to define whose side they think you are on. They will act towards you on the basis of this definition, regardless of your professions."[47] Words may ultimately be futile in convincing offenders who or what one really is. Ultimately, "actions speak louder than words. . . . [T]he researcher will have to demonstrate by . . . actions that he is on the side of the deviants, or at least not on the side of the officials."[48] Police had treated me like just another user and did so with offenders present. This treatment provided the "actions" for me, the picture that spoke a thousand words. Offenders' accounts of my treatment spread rapidly through the grapevine, solidifying my credibility for the remainder of the project, and setting up the snowball sampling procedure I would use to recruit additional respondents.

Why police never attempted to confiscate my notes during these pull-overs, I'll never know. Perhaps it was because they appeared to be indecipherable by anyone but me. Perhaps it was because they didn't reveal anything the cops did not already know or at least thought they knew. Regardless, the law is clearly against ethnographers, who can be held in contempt and sent to jail for protecting sources and withholding information. "There is no privileged relationship between the . . . researcher and his subject similar to that enjoyed by the lawyer and client or psychiatrist and patient."[49] This, of course, says nothing about issues of guilty knowledge or guilty observation. Being aware of dealing operations and watching transactions take place make one an accessory to their commission, a felony whether one participates or not. Criminological fieldworkers almost inevitably will be coconspirators, no matter their motive or intent. "If one is effectively to study adult criminals in their natural settings," Polsky concludes, "he must make the moral decision that in some ways he will break the law himself."[50]

CHAIN REFERRAL AND DATA COLLECTION

The first five respondents were recruited directly from the dealers I initially approached. Four of these five became contacts and provided six additional referrals. Three of these six then referred nine additional respondents. This chain referral method was carried out to secure a forty-person sample. Two contacts in particular proved critical for recruiting work. Snowball samples, after all, are only as good as the gate-keepers on the chain. These two had multiple contacts in the study neighborhood and in neighborhoods nearby with similar characteristics, forms of sales organization, and dealer-customer/dealer-dealer relations. Roughly half of the forty respondents moved in different sets and lived in different parts of the city, providing the opportunity to address the problem that chain referral methods can have in creating a sample of like-minded offenders that offers limited response variance.

Contacts were given eligibility criteria before referring someone to me. Rather broad ranging and reflective of the variable and often vague nature of participation street-level crack dealing involves, these criteria called for someone who trafficked on streets and public thruways one or more days a week, who had done so for at least six months to several different customers per day (six to fifteen), and who grossed between $300 and $2,000 a month from all activity relevant to street crack sales (that is, selling crack, carrying drugs for someone, steering customers, or other assisting activities).[51]

The first set of forty interviews conducted during the summer of 1995 focused on the social organization of street sales as it pertained to risk perception and detection avoidance. An additional fourteen interviews were conducted in the study neighborhood in December 1996. These interviews were structured to explore more systematically the areas that comprise the topical focus of this book—motivation, functions and roles, transactional security, and other core issues in the social organization of streetcorner crack sales. Like Humphreys's "intensive dozen" and Mieczkowski's high-quality sample of fifteen, my "intensive fourteen" provided the richest source of data and primary stock of information on which the present study is based.[52]

Ten of the fourteen were new subjects but similar to the original forty respondents on variables such as age, race, gang membership, amount of crack sold, number of hours per day and per week spent selling it, context in which they sold it, level in the crack distribution hierarchy at which they dealt, and forms of sales activity and social organization in which they participated. I am confident that these fourteen are representative of the original sample and of similar sellers situated in other parts of the city in which streetcorner crack dealing is performed. More on the data's internal and external validity is provided below.

The intensive fourteen's self-reported estimates for the categories listed below were as follows: average gross monthly income per respondent, $1,787; average number of days per week spent selling, six; average grade completion, tenth; average age, 17.5. For the original forty, these estimated averages were as follows: gross monthly income, $2,300; days per week spent selling, 5.5; grade completion, tenth; average age, twenty. Estimations are based on respondent reports and must be interpreted with care, as independent validation of such figures is inherently difficult. All members of the intensive fourteen were African American males. All members of the original forty were African American. Thirty-four of the forty were male, and six were female.

Data were collected using an open-ended interview format guided by specific category and subject headings. This technique allows subjects a measure of latitude and flexibility in their responses. It also helps to make interviews flow much like a conversation, creating a comfort zone between researcher and respondent that facilitates collection of valid and reliable data. Most important, it permits the researcher to study crack sellers without actually becoming one, yielding descriptive data about the dealing subculture and insights into the ways in which sellers "observe, classify, and describe their own life experiences."[53] Interviews were not tape recorded because respondents tended to link recording devices to undercover police. Extensive notes were taken, and further details were filled in immediately after interviews had finished. Interviews took place in private rooms or secluded areas.

Though skeptical at first, interviewees relaxed and opened up soon after interviews had begun. They talked with ease and comfort, apparently trusting the guarantee of anonymity and confidentiality I had given them. Offenders also seemed to enjoy speaking with someone "straight" about their criminal experiences; it may have provided some sort of outlet for them to share their expertise and teach me, someone supposedly "smarter" than them (in terms of academic degrees), a thing or two about street life. As Wright and Decker observe, "The secrecy inherent in criminal work means that offenders have few opportunities to discuss their activities with anyone besides associates, a matter which many find frustrating."[54] Moreover, criminal respondents almost inevitably have certain skills and knowledge that the researcher lacks. This asymmetry may lead them to open up or to open up sooner than they otherwise would. Respondents also may see something in the research that benefits them or define it as an opportunity to correct faulty impressions of what it is they do. Finally, the legitimation from my field contacts was critical; if they told others that it was "cool" to talk to me and that participants would not be "burned" as a result, it tended to be believed.[55]

How reliable and valid are my data? Here I was intruding into the lives of individuals engaged in felonies for which they could receive long sentences. How could I know they were giving me the straight story? How could it have been in their interest to provide incisive, accurate comments about their lives when divulging such details might undermine their success as dealers? To begin, though the inclusion criteria seem fairly straightforward, they are inherently difficult to apply in the real world of street dealing. Some respondents may have lied about their dealing status. Others may have failed to meet the specified eligibility requirements: it seemed a waste, however, to turn away potentially valuable respondents for the sake of adhering to a somewhat arbitrary operational definition of eligibility in the first place. I tried to compensate for possible mistakes by using unobtrusive observational measures—a very revealing strategy. In one case, a respondent interrupted our interview to run to a nearby restroom, so that he could regurgitate two $20 rocks he had swallowed ten minutes before in an attempt to avoid arrest. This is one among a number of such stories. I impressed on my contacts the importance of having referrals meet the criteria and, of course, asked specifically targeted questions designed to screen out those who were inappropriate for the study. That I may not have been able to match every offender to the specified criteria need not be devastating. As Van Maanen notes, imperfections are an inevitable part of fieldwork, given the complexity of the enterprise. Absent evidence of fallibility, the fieldworker may "appear too perfect and thus strain the reader's good faith."[56]

Though participants in the drug market have an image of lying or evading the truth more than others (both nonoffending citizens and other offenders), there is little evidence to support this claim. Self-report data have been carefully assessed by a number of researchers, all of whom conclude that drug dealers are among the best, if not the best, source of information about the behaviors being studied. The most accurate self-report designs are those that ask questions regarding serious criminality and those that involve face-to-face data collection—my technique—rather than surveys administered impersonally. Offender reports are not always immune from "exaggerations, intentional distortions, lies, self-serving rationalizations, or drug-induced forgetfulness," but they may be less susceptible than some might think.[57]

The fact that responses became repetitious indicated sufficient topical coverage, although such repetition could have been an artifact of the sampling design itself. Dealers may have conspired to respond only in a certain way, but their separation from each other in the interview process—both contextually and in many cases over periods of time—makes this unlikely. Reasonable effort was made to question every offender about every issue, but the nature of open-ended qualitative interviewing is such that not all topics could be anticipated and not all offenders could be asked the same questions about issues that emerged later, often serendipitously, during the research process.[58]

The unobtrusive observation I engaged in of drug sales and

interactions among dealers over the twenty-two-month research period, though unsystematic, confirmed many of the
issues reported in the interviews. I have supplemented these
interview and observational data with information collected
during the course of several years of field research on the use,
distribution, and control of street drugs—preceding and including the study period—from persons and places relevant
to the present topic.[59] Eight months of ride-alongs with
officers from an elite gun and drug unit in the St. Louis City
Police Department during 1996 and 1997 form part of this experiential reservoir and inform chapters 3 and 5 in particular.
The researcher is the research instrument in qualitative research, and such experiences can be key to the form, content,
and structure of the work produced.[60]

   As for external validity, the representativeness of a sample
drawn from drug dealers at large in the community—a hidden population—cannot be determined conclusively because
the parameters of the total population are unknown. Region-
specific characteristics of drug markets also are likely to vary
and, accordingly, so will the motivations, social organization,
and transaction-securing techniques sellers use and report. At
the same time, traditional methods—such as household surveys—would not be able to obtain such data in the first place
because they "cannot produce reliable samples," because they
are inefficient, and because most hidden populations are
"rare" (that is, the numbers involved are relatively low).[61]
Even if the present sample cannot be generalized to the total
population of dealers, it nevertheless can significantly expand
our understanding of how urban streetcorner crack dealers
think and act in real-life settings and circumstances. The research setting—St. Louis—also may provide findings gen-
eralizable to a number of cities of similar type, size, and location. This is important. St. Louis is not like New York,
Chicago, Los Angeles, or Miami—the loci of most national
drug research.[62] The city's racial composition (an even black-
white split with virtually no Hispanics), deteriorating socio-
economic conditions, and middle-of-the-country location—

making it geographically removed from primary cocaine supply points, neither a hub nor a source city, yet with an entrenched drug market—render it a uniquely useful research site. Moreover, little research has explored the structures, dynamics, and unique appeal of crack or other drug selling in St. Louis or cities similar to it.[63] The present book attempts to remedy this problem—or at least, to begin to.

The book makes extensive use of quoted material from interview transcripts. It goes without saying that these quotations constitute but a small part of what offenders actually said. As Wright and Decker note, "Selectivity is an unavoidable problem in the textual representation of any aspect of social life—criminal or otherwise—and it would be naive to claim that this cannot distort the resulting manuscript."[64] As is the case with all interview research, some respondents were more helpful than others—either more articulate, informed, knowledgeable, or candid about a particular subject or focal area.[65] Quotes have been chosen to capture the essence of the particular theme or topic under discussion, and every effort has been made to represent them from a wide array of offenders.

Quotes have been edited to meet the textual demands of a manuscript of this nature, but the more colorful and sometimes profane language has been included to provide readers with the flavor and jargon of respondents' statements. Grammar and pronunciation also have been phonetically reproduced in places to provide readers a more intimate feel of offenders' dialect. Bracketed words indicate my own additions or substitutions to explain or amplify comments. Proper names of respondents and the persons and streets they discuss have been changed to meet my promise of anonymity and confidentiality.

2 Motivation

FINANCES AND FAST LIVING

Drastic changes in the post–World War II American economy—deindustrialization and the loss of manufacturing jobs, the increased demand for advanced education and high skills, rapid suburbanization, and the outmigration of middle-class residents—have created chronically depressed inner-city neighborhoods that are home to large numbers of young minority adults who lack a legal source of income. This inability to secure a legal income is the result of larger societal patterns that have reduced the number of accessible decent-paying jobs and created an underclass with few economic options beyond drug selling. Changes in eligibility requirements and reductions in public transfer payments have further undercut the income of marginalized persons in inner-city communities—those at highest risk for street crime. Poverty intensifies their economic and social isolation and fuels their motivation to sell drugs.[1]

Crack dealing emerges for many as the most "proximate and performable" way to meet immediate financial needs.[2] No legal work category allows a person on the first year of the job—without training, socialization, or start-up capital—to earn the kind of money that crack selling provides. And the vast majority of those who deal street crack do not sell every day, most days, or even many hours on the days they do sell. Nonetheless, considerable revenue can be accumulated through part-time sales:[3]

It the money, man. Just see all that money. It daze you, man. Just think what you do with it all. Like my brother [a purportedly big-time crack dealer]. He come in the house with a knot [wad of money] like that. Five g's [$5,000] or somethin'. He said, "You can make this money too." (Jimmy Hat)

I be broke too much. Just sittin' back, no money in your pocket, everyone else got money in they pocket. The money too good [from selling]. (A-Train)

Though crack income may be ephemeral, when it does come, it comes fast and furiously. The cash that could purportedly be made in a short period of time with little effort was attractive:

It's better money than everything. Make twenty dollars in one second, two seconds. It's better than robbery, it's better than everything. I done made three one-hundred-dollar sales in one minute one time. I had just recomped [sic], and some users saw me by my car. I was just gettin' ready to leave [my supplier]. They came up to me, two of 'em did, then we got in and drove for a minute and picked up another [customer] on the way. Drove for a minute and made three one-hundred-dollar sales in one minute. That was three hundred dollars in one minute! (K-Rock)

On the streets money is everything—prized for its power to produce status, respect, and esteem. As anyone who has ever found a $10 bill on a sidewalk knows, even small amounts of cash can feel large when earned quickly with little effort. It is important to note, however, that income from crack sales is almost never as high as sellers report it to be. Though street dealers often brag to outsiders and to one another about how much money they make and how fast they make it, stories of "cocaine wealth" are more mythic than real—based on a few extraordinary sales or past periods when business was booming.[4] The tendency to view things through rose-colored glasses is not unique to street crack sellers. Remembrances generally—and perhaps naturally—shift in a positive or prestige-enhancing direction "for the purpose of allowing us to have a more comfortable recollection [of our life condition]" and to bring autobiographical reconstructions of the past in accord with a person's current status.[5] For each high-level seller who makes exorbitant sums, "the pyramidal nature of drug dealing ensures that there are many hundreds earning" relatively paltry amounts. The revenues earned by most low-level crack sellers are justifiably characterized as "inconsistent," "meager," and "not the stuff from which Mercedes are purchased."[6] Reality is never as wonderful as street offenders make it out to be, but those with no future understandably venerate the past.[7]

Offenders' employability may be the real issue in their choice to sell crack. These offenders are not poster children for the local chamber of commerce or small business association. By and large, they are uneducated, unskilled, crudely mannered, and poorly schooled in the arts of impression management and customer relations; most lack the cultural capital[8] necessary to engage in legitimate business. They are not "nice" in the conventional sense of the term; to be nice is to signal weakness in a world where only the strong survive. The streets are an encapsulated social world enshrouded by conduct norms that "devalue intimacy and label those who express [affect] as weaklings."[9] A number of dealers, not surprisingly, lamented that no one would hire them—forcing their hand, as it were, in the decision to sell crack:

Half the jobs won't hire you. Just like that I heard McDonald's on Lindy, heard they be hiring on the spot. This girl I know, she came in and got her a job. Same day she apply, she got the job. I went in there to apply, and I don't know, I never heard from them. "Why not you hiring?" I said. "Because people already got the job," they told me. I don't know if it was the way I looked or dressed, or maybe they didn't like how I talked. I don't know. (Pee Wee Dancer)

Went lookin' [for work] but nobody call me for jobs. Have to rob, cheat, hustle, and deal [to make any money]. No [legal] money, we gonna have to [sell]. (K-Rock)

Tried to get hired, but [they] never did holler at me. That's what makin' me sell. Sellin' ain't cool, but I see I can't get no job. Don't got nothin' to do but to do it. (Skates)

That the work records of street-level offenders such as these are "sparse, meager, and grossly deficient" is not remarkable.[10] In light of their lack of opportunities—or, more accurately, their woeful unpreparedness for legitimate employment—a number of them waxed responsible about their drug market participation. They claimed to need the money from crack sales to help family members, pay bills, and purchase necessary household items:

I sellin' for a good reason. Give my mama money or buy me some clothes, so she won't gotta buy me stuff all the time and I don't have to ask. I be gettin' older, and I gotta help with the house. My daddy died, and sellin' dope helps with the stress of bills. (Bo Joe)

It's a point of view of what you have to do. I sling to make money on the side—take care of my kid, myself, and my mother. It not a choice. I have to. (Double-D Loc)

I hep my mama with the bills, her car note. She don't even know. I put the money under the bed, in the mattress, or like hide it in the dresser somewhere, and then I go and find it. Look what I found Mama! (Benzo)

I too old to ask my mama for somethin'. I need to be givin' Mama somethin' she need. Dad died two years ago. (Tony Mack)

Such assertions must be taken with a healthy dose of skepticism. Crack revenue is valued first and foremost as a means to achieve respect and status where these are companion qualities and, literally, are worn on one's sleeve. The world of street capitalism dictates that fiscal responsibility be jettisoned and money spent as quickly as it is acquired on material objects that assert status in no uncertain terms. The "material trappings of success" create the "impression of affluence" by which one inevitably is judged:[11]

I seen everyone else with all this jewelry, money, clothes, new cars. I wanted that. My partner who was slingin' had all the stuff I wanted. (Benzo)

Those 5-os [Ford Mustangs] with the phat rims, sounds in 'em
[booming car stereos], goin' to school with g's [thousand dollars]
in your pocket—I wanted to have the same thing. You can't get
no girl with no money. (Tony Mack)

You see who can get the best clothes. Compare to your friends what
you got and what they got. (Short Dog)

Despite all the talk about earning money for big-ticket
items, saving for cars, college, homes, retirement, or other
typically middle-class concerns is noticeably absent. On the
streets, conspicuous consumption is the name of the game,
fueling the competitive pursuit of "personal, nonessential"
items.[12] Expenditures on high-priced commodity goods—
footwear (such as Air Jordans and Air Max Adidas shoes,
which retail for around $150, with new models coming out
every six months or so), clothing (jeans, jackets, sweatshirts,
and shirts from heavily promoted clothing manufacturers
such as Tommy Hilfiger, Guess, Polo, Nautica, Eddie Bauer,
Timberland, and Fasashi that are sold at prices ranging from
$40 to $250), and accessory items (earrings, gold-capped
teeth, and gold chains at $100 to a few hundred dollars
each)—become a means to this end. Such purchases demonstrate a "cool transcendence"[13] over the financial concerns
that plague most everyone else. Through display, the wearer
can proclaim himself "to be someone who has overcome—if
only temporarily—the financial difficulties faced by others
on the streetcorner."[14]

The irony of this display of the very accouterments of cultural capital that might enable offenders to pass[15] in the legal
economy is striking. Yet there is nothing unusual about engaging in illegitimate enterprise to purchase products that
represent the essence of respectable coolness. The paradox is
that dealers are in no position to apply these symbols where
they would do them any "legitimate" good. Moreover, their
clothes often are soiled and smelly and worn to serve emaciated crack addicts in front of burned-out tenements and litter-
strewn vacant lots. But regardless of their condition, on the
streets such items have immediate symbolic value—so much

so that predators treat the "display of wealth" by others as a "personal affront that should not go unpunished." [16] Indeed, it is not unusual for armed robberies of those perceived to be "high-catting"—that is, showing off by wearing expensive status items—to result in the robbers wearing the stolen items.

Seen through the eyes of mainstream America, the offenders' preoccupation with "fly clothes" and high fashion seems immature, irrational, or pathological.[17] Yet to the dealers, it makes perfect sense. People need shoes, shirts, jackets, and jeans, but these offenders require the gold-standard version. On the streets, to go cheap on one's appearance is to discount one's reputation. Desires get warped into needs through a subtle but powerful process of self-deception, in which the "ostentatious enjoyment and display of luxury items" comes to take precedence over most everything else.[18] To spend with reckless abandon, therefore, becomes natural and expected as anomic self-indulgence quickly takes on a life of its own.

Such habits are intensified by the fact that money earned illegally holds "less intrinsic value" than cash secured through legitimate work. As already noted, the way money is obtained is a "powerful determinant of how it is defined, husbanded, and spent."[19] The sought-after clothing and accessory manufacturers feed such habits by frequently changing their products in small but significant ways to make rapidly obsolete gear that was once cutting-edge. Such strategies exploit a particular way of thinking on the streets, and, as cultural trend setters, street-culture participants become caught in a cycle they may not understand but feel they must join lest they be labeled as losers.[20] It is but another way in which the economic mandates of modern American capitalism exploit those who can least afford it.

The lack of fiscal responsibility often means that the offenders will be penniless despite an extended career of selling drugs.[21] That most street sellers "subsist at a very low level of economic well-being," even though the revenues they generate greatly exceed federal poverty levels and could provide "a comfortable middle-class existence," is not surprising.[22]

A number of respondents explained that they made large amounts of cash but had virtually nothing to show for it later—beyond high-priced commodity goods that had long since lost their value. "I ain't have the shit I used to," K-Rock lamented. "I was makin' all this money, saved $30,000. [Now I have nothing.] I don't know what the fuck happened. I had this much money [motioning], all this grip. Felt like I was rich." The modest interview payment I provided was accepted by most offenders with an eagerness that betrayed their woeful financial condition.

Adding to these offenders' fiscal nightmare, the meaning of fast living has changed dramatically since the mid-1980s in both the type and magnitude of wealth necessary to support it.[23] As demand for their product continues to decline, streetcorner crack dealers are finding it increasingly difficult to live up to the material standards set by their predecessors. Undoubtedly, this motivates them to relish fast money even more, entrenching them deeper and deeper in its pursuit to buy increasingly unattainable status items—items that become more valuable as a result of their unattainability.[24] To be sure, offenders' spending habits are both cause and effect of their persisting poverty. Yet the tendency to overspend earnings is not remarkable in an economy that fetishizes material goods: crack sellers are simply a "caricaturally visible version" of a "very North American phenomenon."[25] What middle-class high school student has not spent money on the latest fashion trend—whether Calvin Klein platform shoes, Guess jeans, or a Tommy Hilfiger jacket—to the detriment of his or her college savings? Against this backdrop, offenders can only wax nostalgic of days gone by when crack was in high demand and cash was abundant.

AUTONOMY

The cultural ethos of the streetcorner renders any form of subordination unacceptable. This ethos is part of a larger resentment of authority, external control, and restrictions on behavior that many street offenders feel deeply. Freedom from subservience and the latitude to do what one wants, when one wants to do it, is critical in a life defined by structural subordination and the desire for both practical and symbolic emancipation. On the purely subjective side, obedience to the norms of the legal economy contradicts "street culture's definition of personal dignity—especially for males who are socialized not to accept public subordination."[26] To be cool, one must not be under anyone else's thumb.

Crack selling offers "leisurely" and more profitable work in which offenders can determine their own hours, work patterns, and related occupational habits. Working a normal job, by contrast, requires a person to take orders, conform to a schedule, minimize informal peer interaction, show up sober and alert, and restrict one's freedom of movement for a specified period of time. Such requirements are not acceptable to many of the sellers in my sample.

Describing the perceived benefits of crack selling, several offenders used fast-food jobs as the comparative standard— illustrative in its own right.

I just be out here bullshittin'. Don't take no orders from no motherfucker. I make just as much as this motherfucker in Hardees. I make more than that. I make three Hardees checks in one day! Get all the freedom you want. Ain't gotta be in no certain [fixed and unchanging] spot. Go where you wanna go. (Fade)

Autonomy was even more important given the offenders' predilection for indolence. Although streetcorner crack sellers desire the rewards offered by society, they are often too lazy to pursue them through legitimate channels. "I'm lazy. I don't want no job," Deuce Low explained. Or as Short Dog put it, "The money [good], and it's easy. Been doin' it for six years, five hours a day, five days a week. It's plain old easy for real." "I like slingin' 'cause I'm free," added Ice-D. "Can hang with my partners, drink, whatever, have fun. If I be workin' at Rally's, I think about what my partners doin'—if they be blowed [high on marijuana], if they havin' fun. I gots to be workin' all the while." Normal jobs were considered "too hard" and not worth the effort, given the separation of work from reward in space and time. Industry and ambition give way to sloth and avarice, and like water running down the hill, the offenders take the path of least resistance.[27] "I'm addicted to slinging," concluded Pee Wee Dancer. "I'm gonna do it 'til I die." For Jimmy Hat, crack selling becomes "really all the money in this world," the most convenient and autonomous way he can achieve "extrinsically defined success as quickly as possible."[28]

Whether selling streetcorner crack is "addictive," as Pee Wee Dancer implies, or "seductive" and "thrilling," as other research suggests, is questionable. A number of studies paint a rosier picture than may be warranted, suggesting that drug selling provides feelings of excitement that revolve around participation in illicit enterprise, hustling, scamming, and evading the authorities. The adrenaline-pumping danger, joys of hustling and getting over, and challenges of trying to outfox antagonists in games with zero-sum outcomes are said to be powerfully seductive lures for those who thrive on excitement. To sell drugs, these studies suggest, is to amplify the moment and to differentiate one's existence "from the humdrum routine of daily life."[29]

Despite the findings of these studies, no respondents claimed fun or excitement to be their primary motivating force in the decision to sell crack. This is understandable. Curbside crack selling, after all, *is* overwhelmingly boring, tedious, and routine.[30] Long hours are spent essentially doing nothing, and, very often, offenders would rather be doing something else. Much of the time spent "selling" is really spent waiting for something to happen. As Deuce Low put it, "It's only excitin' when the money comin' in. Other than that . . . gotta keep and hold [the dope] if there ain't no money comin' in. Never know when the money gonna come." Working conditions in the crack trade also are often far inferior to what these same sellers might experience in the legitimate economy. In the minds of the sellers, it is always a crisp fall day or balmy, moonlit summer night; the reality is far different. Sellers ply their trade in extremes of weather, in the dark of night, in bitter cold and oppressive humidity, for hours on end. It is only the *perception* of fast money for little effort, the opportunity to "hang out" freely with peers and party while working, and the lack of realistically available alternative occupations that offer similar benefits, which prevent curbside crack selling from becoming wholly unacceptable.[31]

USER-DEALERS?

Historically, the opportunity to party has been presumed to be the main reason that most sellers choose to sell drugs in the first place—that is, they can have a readily available stash from which to partake. The lower one descends in dealing hierarchies, the more likely this is to be the case. This is particularly true for crack: those who use (smoke) the product (crack) that they sell are forever cannibalizing their own supply, jeopardizing any chance they might have to move up the dealing ladder or to stay up there very long. To no one's surprise, the paradigm of the "purely economic entrepreneur" whose participation in street crack dealing is "solely fiscal" lacks empirical support. By an overwhelming margin, dealers who use dominate the street crack scene.[32]

Even so, no respondents admitted using the crack they sold. Typically, offenders attributed their alleged teetotaling to crack's "pharmacological omnipotence," the effects of which are thought to be so powerful and short-acting that it addicts very quickly those who try it and makes the financial resources required to sustain use boundless.[33] The majority of offenders claimed that one experimental hit would risk a lifetime of addiction:

I ain't messin' wit' that. Get sprung or somethin' [start an all-consuming addiction]. Don't ever wanna start off like that for real. (Jimmy Hat)

That shit [crack] tacky as a motherfucker. I don't fuck with it. Don't like that smell. Just sell it and go. That shit smell like a motherfuckin' dead man. . . . I seen the effects of that shit on the younger

generation [people who started using in the 1980s]. I could pretty
easily be the same person I'm serving twenty years from now.
(Fade)

If I try, I be addicted. I just be sellin' it. (Pee Wee Dancer)

Skates insisted that crack was a "whole different thing. I'll
smoke dips [blunts—cigars emptied of tobacco and refilled
with marijuana—dunked in PCP] 'fore I smoke crack. It
[dips] don't have you out there ready to rob, kill people." He
implied that crack, unlike other drugs, increased vulnerability
to predators because the singular focus on getting high pre-
cluded adequate attention to the business at hand. "[Not
smoking crack] let me keep my p's and q's, my head high, so I
can be lookin' around, watchin' my back." There is support for
his contention in the literature. As Shover and Honaker note,
inebriation can make legal threats appear to be "remote and
improbable contingencies" that one needn't bother with or
fret over.[34] Moreover, inebriation can make the difference between seeing predators or the police in time to escape or being
"dazzled for a fatal instant."[35] These and other issues relevant
to avoiding apprehension are explored in depth in chapters 5
and 6.

There may be some truth to offenders' alleged teetotaling,
discrepant as it may be in relation to what we know about low-
level crack sellers' drug-use patterns. Urban minority youth
across the country report the devastating impact crack has had
on their parents, siblings, other relatives, and friends and vow
never to follow the same road. They see firsthand its debilitating effects on those who use—the humiliating sex acts (a
"blow job" can be had on many urban streetcorners for $3 to
$5, the "whole nine yards" for $10 or less), the "unstoppable
missions" to generate funds to keep binges going, and other
such demoralizing activities. Crackheads have been likened to
"walking human carcasses," a label that graphically depicts
the emaciation and wasting that accompanies compulsive use
at the expense of proper nutrition and personal hygiene.[36]
Sellers have witnessed this personal devastation up close—at
street level and in a declining market, where crack's effects of-

ten are most acute—since the users who remain often represent the worst of the worst:

I seen what crack can do. Some customers be out there sellin' trash bags, stealin', robbin'. I don't wanna be in they predicament. I see how they be comin' to me, askin' for credit, they be all desperate, geekin', messed up. I don't wanna be like that. (Double-D Loc)

They be walkin' all night geekin', be crazy, zombielike. . . . Don't care about they kids. . . . All they wanna do is smoke. (Tony Mack)

Dope fiends runnin' around [saying], "Can I borrow twenty-five cents, fifty cents?" from people. Then they come to the sell man with all that shit all rolled up to get more. (Jimmy Hat)

Tony Mack's own sister had a particularly voracious appetite for crack, so extreme that he and his family had reportedly disowned her:

I don't even think of her bein' in my family no more. She steal clothes from my family. Every time I get some money, I gotta be hidin' it. She robbed me four hundred dollars yesterday [that he made from crack sales].

Intriguingly, some offenders' negative opinions about crack mutated into a twisted sense of guilt:

You think about they mama, daddy. What if they be smokin' like that? Like givin' rocks [crack] to another dude's mama. (Jimmy Hat)

Smoke around me, it hurt my feelin's. I hate that, when I be sellin' and when he smoke in my face. I feel ashamed, [gotta] walk away. (Pee Wee Dancer)

You sellin' and you know you be hurtin' somebody else mama, parent, but if they stupid enough to do it, go on and let 'em. That's how people be thinkin'. (Bo Joe)

I shouldn't be doin' it. I hurtin' some other motherfucker's mama, daddy. They love they mama just like I love my mama. Can't hep they motha wanta smoke that shit. Don't no motherfucker want they mama to smoke. Hurt the shit outta me if it was my mother. It be like one of my friends sellin' shit to my mama. I ain't gonna like that shit either. (Fade)

To claim that these offenders didn't "party," however, would be misleading. Youths in general and gang members in particular spend the majority of their time in groups, and what those groups usually do together is drink alcohol and do drugs. Such a finding has been replicated in a diversity of contexts and historical eras.[37] As impulsive sensation seekers in search of immediate gratification, party pursuits were integral to the offenders' lifestyle and comprised an overarching appeal of street culture itself. Alcohol—especially fortified beverages such as Colt 45, Thunderbird, MD 20-20—and marijuana (not crack), however, were offenders' reported drugs of choice.

Getting high on marijuana was preferred, with offenders frequently smoking oversized blunts that delivered a potent and long-lasting buzz. As A-Train put it, "If it ain't weed, I ain't smokin' nothin' else. No water [PCP], no hair-ron [heroin], none o' that. It ain't me. It ain't me trying to bring myself down like that." Marijuana use carries none of crack's stigma and, indeed, has been glorified in many inner-city communities by the rappers and celebrities many central-city street youth most admire. Marijuana also is perceived to be neither "bad," harmful, nor illegal. K-Rock anointed weed as "medicine," claiming that "hospitals use it"—a vague political reference to its 1996 medical legalization in Arizona and California. Recent Drug Use Forecasting data indicate the widespread nature of cannabis use, particularly among youthful offenders in central cities.[38] For the first time in five years, the percentage of urban arrestees testing positive for marijuana is equal to or greater than the percentage testing positive for cocaine in thirteen of the twenty-four DUF cities—including St. Louis.[39] As one respondent summarized:

Everybody smoke bo [weed]. From an eleven-year-old on up to grandmas and grandpas. You know somethin'? My grandma probably the only one around I know who don't smoke it.

As a leisure drug, weed is perceived by dealers to be relaxing, innocuous, and a good way to pass the time while selling. It also is an economical high because a person can get sufficiently buzzed with an amount worth $10 or less and have the high last for several hours. Tolerance and physiological dependence are rare—an important plus—so that persons discontinuing its use do not experience withdrawal symptoms.[40] Enforcement of marijuana possession and use laws also is lax, motivating offenders to branch off into marijuana sales when crack sales are slow. Weed, explained Skates, is not "as illegal as crack." Trey Tone added, "Poh-lice really don't trip off weed like they do crack. Ain't that big o' deal. Gotta get caught with weight."

Some offenders undoubtedly were lying about using marijuana to the exclusion of crack. Drug dealers almost invariably are users of the drug they sell, whether that drug is marijuana, cocaine powder, heroin, or crack.[41] The widely believed stereotype of a drug seller as someone who sells drugs that he seldom uses is largely unsupported by available evidence.[42] Some research does suggest very limited crack use among adolescents who deal it, but such a pattern is short-lived. Most eventually do become heavy users.[43] One of my respondents followed exactly this progression. Unfortunately, I found this out only after he robbed me at gunpoint of $50 to finance his burgeoning habit. When all is said and done, the "provocative image of the well-disciplined dealer, whose motivations are exclusively financial and who abstains from drug use to maximize his or her dealing skills, has no grounding."[44]

It should be noted, however, that gang-affiliated crack sellers may be more insulated from crack use than others with similar access to the drug. The normative proscriptions against drug use (except marijuana)—and crack use in particular—in gangs have been duly noted. That peers tend to be the most influential factor in determining one's likelihood to use drugs—and determining the drug of choice in the event drugs are used—also is well documented. Moreover, a considerable body of evidence demonstrates that rates of drug use—including alcohol, cigarettes, pills, hallucinogens, cocaine, and heroin (but excluding marijuana)—tend to be lowest among African American adolescents. Teetotaling also is important to business because drug use impairs one's ability to run one's operations. Being your own best customer is a sure formula for disaster, "so [gang-affiliated] drug dealers, who have as much access to the drug as anyone, [may be] able to defer its gratifications in the interests of doing business."[45] Whatever the ultimate truth, dealers' reported refusal to take part in using what they sold is instructive in reflecting expectations of conduct—if not the conduct itself.

CONCLUSION

By offering the promise of easy cash and fast living to those who venture into its ranks, crack selling attracts young workers away from the low-paying, dead-end jobs the legal economy offers. But although it often is more lucrative than legitimate employment, crack dealing does not launch sellers on the path to lucrative and sustained incomes. This is particularly true when all its costs are considered—finding the supplier who offers the best price, packaging the dope, waiting for customers (increasingly in vain), tracking down buyers for overdue loans, serving jail time—in addition to the emotional costs incurred through worrying about being caught, robbed, or killed.

The decision to sell crack on the corner may reflect resignation more than anything else. Given that nothing else can equal the income and work conditions crack sales are perceived to provide, even in a declining market the choice to deal becomes relatively easy. The universe of money-making crimes from which these offenders realistically can pick is limited. They do not hold jobs that would allow them to violate even a low-level position of financial trust. Nor do they possess the technical know-how to commit lucrative commercial break-ins or the interpersonal skills needed to perpetrate successful frauds.[46] Burglary—another possible option—is time-consuming and risky and requires the booty to be fenced before one gets paid. Robbery requires a stomach for violence that many street offenders brag about having but, in reality, lack. Although offenders will not ignore emergent criminal opportunities and indeed can exercise versatility when the occasion calls for it, drug dealing is a main-line offense they are likely to turn to first.

Requiring little skill, training, or start-up time, selling crack becomes the most "proximate and performable" way[47] to alleviate financial pressures in a world that no longer provides a legal means to net the same perceived rewards per unit of time and effort expended. Yet crack selling is much like any other business. To be successful requires prudence, forethought, planning, and preparation. Given the propensity for crack dealers to ignore these requirements, a dilemma arises: dealers gravitate to crack selling for the freedoms it provides, yet to enjoy these freedoms they must be responsible and prudent enough to be able to continue selling. This paradox says a lot about why these offenders are on the streets in the first place and why they are likely to stay there.

As macroscopic obstacles—such as poverty and urban decay—continue to mount, the offenders' hedonistic pursuit of self-indulgence is likely to continue. This pursuit becomes both a response to, and a justification for, continued life on the street. The "enjoyment of 'good times'" and minimal concern for obligations and commitments "external to [one's] immediate social setting" are attractive for those seeking pleasure in a largely pleasureless world.[48] But as much as these offenders may have sought liberation through the pursuit of instant gratification, this quest ultimately is both self-defeating and subordinating. Those enmeshed in street life may never see it this way, but objective assessments of reality are difficult to render when is rationality as severely delimited as it is here. Suffice to say that, for those in my sample, "choices" occur in a context where not only rationality is sharply bounded, but it barely exists. If one takes the influence of context seriously, then most sellers make decisions in a social and psychological terrain bereft of realistic alternatives.[49] Life on the street effectively obliterates—or at least severely circumscribes—the range of objectively available options, so much so as to be almost deterministic. Offenders typically are overwhelmed by their own predicament—structural, financial, emotional, and otherwise—and may see drug-market participation as the only option. Chronic isolation from conventional others and lifestyles only reinforces their insularity.[50] As their behavior takes on a self-enclosed quality, alternatives come to look less and less feasible or practical. Offenders get locked deeper and deeper into a downward life trajectory.[51]

3 Social Organization

Though crack is legally proscribed—a "tarnished good"[1]—it is bought and sold in the marketplace like any other good. The crack market, however, has certain distinguishing characteristics. There is constant exposure to violence. Transactions are highly vulnerable to exploitation. Duplicity on the part of customers and sellers is so common as to be institutionalized. Overall, instability reigns, and predatory arrangements thrive between actors at all levels.[2]

A freelance system of distribution dominates the St. Louis street crack scene, as it does most urban drug markets. Scholars had predicted that this system—with its individualistic, every-man-for-himself orientation—would weaken, or perhaps even disappear, over time. As demand became more established and competition increasingly virulent, crack markets were thought likely to become hierarchically organized as a precondition to survival. Freelancers would form loose confederations and ultimately "vertical business" operations characterized by pooled interdependence, vertical differentiation, and well-defined employer-employee relationships.[3] Recognizing that vertical business models are ideal-types, nothing approaching an evolution has occurred in St. Louis. Although open-air, curbside crack sellers no longer predominate, those who remain face both a mature demand and predatory competition and yet, arguably, are the least organized dealing stratum of any drug market.

COPPING ONE'S SUPPLY

In any retail enterprise, merchandising is impossible without first procuring a product to sell. Though street gangs neither direct nor control street crack distribution, gang membership provides affiliated sellers access to a supply and the connections necessary to do business.[4] For the majority of offenders in my sample, suppliers were ubiquitous and easily accessible. They typically were older brothers, cousins, and other sellers within a particular gang-affiliated drug set or persons affiliated with a friendly gang constellation nearby. Customary purchases were fifties ($50 worth of crack wholesale, about a gram), boppers ($100 of crack wholesale, about two grams or ten $20 rocks), quarter ounces ($250 wholesale), and, less frequently, half-ounces ($500 wholesale). Fifties and boppers comprise the modal purchases and generally could be bought within the neighborhood.

Price and quality, though fairly uniform, varied enough so that sellers had an incentive to shop around. Convenience was overriding, but if individual sellers thought they could readily get a better "play," they would look for it. As Prus notes, buyers want a good product at a fair price, but "buying is far from a static or simple dollars and cents exchange." It requires a degree of "reflective planning" and is "strikingly qualified" by the activities of those whose services buyers seek.[5] Sellers who are able to keep abreast of prices, quantities, and locations of suppliers stood to make the best deals. Social organization is about information—about who knows what and how to use that knowledge to advantage.[6]

Though commonplace in the heroin and cocaine powder eras of the 1960s, 1970s, and early 1980s, buying on consignment is not customary among street-level crack distributors.[7] By and large, the dealers in my sample were reticent about asking to be fronted and reportedly would do so only when necessary. This kind of dependence means owing somebody something, since "assistance of any type is limited and has reciprocal costs."[8] Self-reliance, by contrast, "earns for offenders a measure of respect from peers for their demonstrated ability to 'get over'."[9] As Bo Joe put it, "I don't let somebody front me 'cause if it don't come out the way it supposed to be, you don't get your money, he don't get his money. . . . It's all just a big commotion between you and your friends."

Sellers typically purchase their supply already rocked up. To rock it up oneself required time and effort, access to a kitchen, and the know-how to manufacture the product correctly—a skill not all sellers possess. As Fade explained, "It's best to get the shit hard. They [suppliers] already know how much to put in of what—how to cut it up, how much water and all that." Crack can be rocked up in any number of ways, but each requires boiling water and baking soda to bind with the cocaine and free it from its hydrochloride salt.[10] A variety of comeback agents—baby laxative, inositol, or milk sugar, for example—can be mixed in during the cooking process to increase the volume of the product while retaining the drug's psychoactive effect, thereby making individual sales more profitable. In powder form, the quality of cocaine also can be quite difficult to gauge. Any number of nonpsychoactive cutting agents (such as lidocaine or procaine) can be added after the cooking process is complete to mimic the texture, taste, color, and numbing sensation produced by cocaine hydrochloride.

Though buying is always a gamble—taking place in a setting of "shifting uncertainties" and reflecting dependencies on others outside the exchange process[11]—procuring a prefabricated product eased sellers' fears of being swindled. Nonetheless, inexperienced sellers benefited from bringing smokers with them to verify a purchase's authenticity. More seasoned vendors did not bother with "tasters" because they were able to discern product quality by smell, touch, and sight. Good crack has a yellowish or off-white tinge, is hard but brittle, and has a characteristic odor—even before heat is applied.

After purchasing their "bundle," the sellers package individual quantities for retail, typically by cutting out the corners of sandwich baggies, placing rocks of particular sizes inside, and knotting each end—and sometimes burning the ends for extra closure. In these tightly knotted balls, rocks can easily be swallowed or spat out in the event of a police chase. Meanwhile, excess inventory can be buried in secret places and protected from the elements. The packaging process is more often than not imprecise, with quantities typically eyed rather than scaled (though some sellers did weigh individual retail units). The denomination packaged and sold by those in the sample generally depended on how much a given dealer purchased at any one time. A bopper purchased wholesale, for example, might be broken down into ten $20 rocks—yielding $200 in sales, or double the initial investment. Quarter-ounces purchased wholesale for $250 might be broken down into some combination of fifties, twenties, and tens that equaled, when retailed, $500. Half-ounces purchased wholesale for $500 might be broken down into boppers, fifties, and twenties equal to $1,000 at retail.

The goal is to double one's money. More often than not, this is a goal and nothing more. As K-Rock explained, "The only way to double your money like that for real is to sell twenties. You need all twenty sales to make a straight profit." On the street, dealers confront desperate and financially strapped users wanting to "get over"—soliciting twenties for $12, fifties for $40, or tens for $3 or $4. Buyers would sometimes reportedly bring the full amount to a transaction and attempt to either hide this fact or, more brazenly, ask for change from the dealers they were trying to short (for example, to purchase alcohol or cigarettes to temper the inevitable crash). To maintain profit margins, dealers might bite open a baggie, break off the quantity requested, and sell the remainder later for its marginal value—or even better, at full price to some dupe. Breaking off pieces, however, is inconvenient, imprecise, messy (crumbs might be dropped), and time-consuming. In the meantime, the sale might be lost to competition or, worse yet, observed by police.

To avoid this, a small number of $5 and $10 rocks might be prepackaged. Such nickel and dime sales, however—referred to on the streets of some cities as "kibbles and bits"—were disliked.[12] Like most merchants, crack sellers want to make the fewest sales for the most money. This is particularly true for streetcorner dealers, whose lifestyle and risk of arrest make less work better: fewer transactions for larger amounts reduce the chances of arrest and allow the sellers to dedicate more time to purely hedonistic pursuits.

The frequency with which sellers purchased supplies varied by the individual. As a general rule, most reported trying to time their purchases to coincide with periods of high demand—typically on, or shortly before, the first of the month (with the influx of public transfer payments). Social security, AFDC, and disability checks are in the several-hundred-dollar range, and sellers reportedly could expect to pocket a significant portion of these amounts from customers. "It be poppin' on the first, people be buyin' fifties [not just fives, tens, and twenties]," Pee Wee Dancer remarked. "On the first, everybody wanta make some money." "The set be deep," continued Deuce Low. "Everybody be outside. Everybody tryin' to get their issue off. Everybody tryin' to get their ends on." "You make a killin' [around the first]," concluded Skates. To not have crack when public transfer money hit the streets would be to forgo potentially substantial profits. As Bourgois et al. observe, the illicit drug economy is facilitated and energized by the very institutions of government that seek to suppress and inhibit illicit drug use.[13] Recent welfare reform legislation is intended to address this problem by reducing the amount of transfer money and altering its form so as to make it less liquid.

After the arrival of government checks, ending with food stamp allotments on the fifteenth of the month, demand reportedly drops off. A number of offenders claim to branch off into marijuana sales to maintain cash flow and to generate additional funds to invest in crack purchases before the next cycle of public transfer payments. Though product diversification may complicate matters, it can generate interest in a seller's other goods—crack, in this case—that is beneficial when these sales become more frequent and lucrative (near the first of the month). More important, product diversification hedges the overall market risk and increases the likelihood that one will sell "something," no matter how slow things get.[14]

As noted in chapter 2, the popularity of marijuana has skyrocketed in recent years. Weed sales reportedly are quite profitable. For $100, at the time of this research, a seller could purchase an ounce or "zo" and package it into an assortment of $5 and $10 blunts—sometimes dunking them in "water" (PCP) to sell them as "dips" or rolling them with sprinkled crack to sell them as chewy blunts, primos, or woolas. Blunt sales typically resulted in a 50 to 80 percent return on the investment. Moreover, weed is perceived to sell regardless of the time of month. "Crack is more money [a lot of sales at one time]," Tony Mack explained, "but weed sell faster [you make sales all the time, so] you make more money with weed."

Criminal sanctions were correctly perceived to be much less severe for marijuana than for crack, allowing income supplementation and risk reduction at the same time. In St. Louis, as in many other metropolitan jurisdictions around the country, criminal statutes for minor marijuana possession are weak. Any quantity under 35 grams carries a misdemeanor charge; anything over, a felony. Considerably more than 35 grams is generally necessary to get circuit attorneys to proceed with a case. Police often are reluctant to enforce marijuana possession statutes to begin with, diluting further the threat of sanctions. As Skates remarked, "Weed ain't that illegal like dope is. They [police] catch you with a gang of dope [crack], they send you up to penitentiary. They catch you with blunts, they say, 'Don't lemme catch you with no more of this.' Then they let you go."

Whether or not dealers sold marijuana in down times, always having crack to sell, regardless of the time of the month, seemed to be their most profitable strategy. As Prus notes, profits, more than anything else, hinge on having merchandise available when customers want it.[15] Customers will seek out the most reliable and well-stocked suppliers first—especially when the commodity involved is criminally sanctioned, high risk, and hard to obtain. Those wise enough to maintain a baseline supply stood to capture the sales that did come through—no matter how meager or intermittent they were. By and large, however, most offenders were neither well stocked nor reliable. They lived for the moment, were lazy, and were largely incapable of engaging in the kind of cost accounting that permitted maintenance of baseline inventories. This undermines attempts to cultivate a stable cadre of brand-loyal customers, as is shown shortly.

STREET SELLING

Consistent with previous research on gang-affiliated drug sellers,[16] those in my sample typically sold by themselves, in pairs, in trios, or in slightly larger groups of four to six individuals within the study neighborhood. Individuals or cliques of sellers were sprinkled throughout the area and set up shop on corners and vacant lot fronts. No formal rules dictated where or when a particular person or clique could establish itself—though certain sellers were more likely to be found on certain streets, corners, or housefronts. There also did not appear to be any hierarchical role interdependence, role specificity, or functional division of labor—three important operational measures of organization. As A-Train and Deuce Low observed, respectively:

We sell by ourself, but we all out together. But everybody sellin' for they self. My partners, they all be outside, but I'm not really slingin' with them. Anywhere I stand, somebody gonna be 'round, [but I sell by myself].

Each individual in they own area, but we all as one. It's like a family. . . . [But] everybody tryin' to get their issue off, everybody tryin' to get their ends on [trying to make money]. Nobody answer to nobody. Everyone equal.

Though instances of rudimentary employer-employee relations were reported (where one dealer might "kick down" money or drugs to one or more others in return for their serving as couriers, servers, informal lookouts, or protectors), such practices were infrequent and episodic. Sellers simply were not cohesive or organized enough to establish formal or lasting role structures. Youthful street sellers—particularly gang-affiliated ones—are not bound by feelings of loyalty, duty, or solidarity. They tend to hold each other in low esteem, and their relationships hinge on aggression, mutual insult, and the pervasive need to assert and protect their status. Such qualities are not conducive to the formation of internally cohesive or interdependent functioning drug-selling groups.[17]

More often than not, group forms of selling were disordered, chaotic, and predatory—"with lots of individuals involved and little coherence to the tasks involved."[18] Indeed, the only group behavior seemed to be competing individuals joined at one place and time. This is illustrated best by the two modal forms of group orientation that did emerge—"get 'em, got 'em" and the "bum rush."

Get 'em, got 'em was the more innocuous of the two. In this game, dealers competed to see who could spot the user first and thus get the sale first. Whoever saw the user first "got" the sale—hence "get 'em, got 'em." As one respondent explained:

You be sittin' on the set and everybody be lookin' up the street for the dope fiend. 'Cause when he come, the first one who see him yells, "Got 'em!" and they get the sale.

Sales were tied directly to acuity in spotting customers. There appeared to be no limit to the number of sales any seller could procure consecutively. Of course, the more consecutive sales a dealer got, the more quickly he would sell out and be removed from the competition, opening up opportunities for those less attentive, creating a natural check of sorts.

Bum rushes, the second and more common form of group orientation, were an animated and physically aggressive version of get 'em, got 'em. In this competition, at least two sellers—but usually more—would make an entrepreneurial windsprint to a newly spotted customer. Whoever arrived first would get the sale or, at least, would be in the best position to get it. The more desperate for money one or more sellers were, and the more of them convened in space and time, the more prone to bum rushing they appeared to become. As A-Train put it, "It be like ants tryin' to get a piece of crumb." Desperation was not the only prerequisite. Certain sellers are prone to hog customers, so the presence of one greedy seller might be all it takes to start a stampede. Bum rushes represent collective retail behavior at its worst, a kind of mindless action that is the epitome of free expression yet one that also is inherently threatening to individuality.[19]

Like get 'em, got 'em, bum rushing appeared to have a point that naturally checked the number of sellers who viably could participate: after a certain number of sellers had spotted a dope fiend and began rushing toward him, it soon became futile for more to do so. As Ice-D explained:

> We see a customer, five'll start runnin' to get 'em. By time those five do, five more will just stand back and look. It's like, "Forget it. I get the next one [sale]." 'Cause too much trouble [to run after everybody else already has], and you probably not get the sale anyway—damn too many [sellers there] already.

Being surrounded by a throng of hucksters, all proclaiming the superiority of *their* product, spitting rocks into their hands, clutching rocks with a death grip, shoving each other out of the way, and jostling the buyer in the process, is no doubt disconcerting to the potential buyer. The buyer does not know whom to deal with, who is selling the real thing and who is not, whose rocks are the biggest, whose rocks just look bigger by virtue of clever packaging, and if or when police will appear. All of this may occur in a context in which the buyer is crashing from a recent binge or is paranoid from ongoing use—adding to the aura of chaos. Transacting with the first seller on the scene—though expeditious—is not necessarily wise. Gankers—dealers who sell hardened wax, peanuts, velamints, and almonds—can be, and often are, the first ones to reach a prospective customer. Taking the first stone offered may allow users to leave the area quickly and reduce their risk of arrest, but they might not come away with the real thing. A better deal might be forthcoming with a little patience. Then again, patience is a scarce commodity on the streets— particularly given a customer's precarious psychological state coupled with the ever-present threat of being caught. Bum rushes create an indisputable dilemma, requiring the most scrutiny of the merchandise yet affording the least opportunity to do so.

It is also easy to see how a buyer, mobbed by a frenzied swarm of street youths with ambiguous and perhaps ominous intentions, might misinterpret the bum rush as "an attack." As Tony Mack mused,

Dope fiend see a gang of people runnin' at 'em, they think you fixing to rob 'em. Sometimes, they get scared like that and run off [before sellers are even copresent with them]. Not a lot of dope fiends comin' through [any more], and the ones that do, they be gettin' rushed by like five or six dudes.

Bum rushes were not all that well liked by sellers either. Rushing is indiscreet, obtrusive, and risky. "Negotiation" with users on the open street (brief as it may be), comparing stones with those of other dealers, and "cajoling" users to purchase their stones takes time and generates a commotion. This notwithstanding, the desperation to beat everyone else to the buyers made those first to arrive most vulnerable to victimization, since they could not always be sure of whom or what they were running up to.

Bo Joe and K-Rock understood that the lifeblood of bum rushes—greed—was potentially counterproductive. "You ain't gonna get nowhere tryin' to be greedy," said the former. "You try to be greedy," K-Rock added, "you try to get all the money, you get caught up. Can't be greedy in this business [and do it for long]." Greed is lust, and lust can destroy caution as one's "intellectual sentries" are overwhelmed.[20]

At the same time, even greedy freelancers are capable of working out marketing arrangements "amicably, with little competition or violence."[21] As Johnson et al. observe, "freelance sellers may obtain their supplies independently of each other, [but they may also] make 'gentleman's agreements' not to compete for customers, territory, or prices in a specific locale."[22] The rotation system was as close as the sellers got to establishing amicable marketing relations. Rotations involved the unsophisticated practice of taking turns:

You take turns. I get a sale, then another one'll [customer] pull up and it they [others'] turn. If they be six people on the block, you just go one, two, three, four, five, six and start all over after that. Person out the longest get the next sale.   (Trey Tone)

Rotations, however, were reported infrequently, seldom observed, and generally more the exception than the rule. They appeared most likely to be used when a number of sellers had enough dope to sell and enough customers to sell to, and a particular selling clique was egalitarian enough to allow sharing—an uncommon state of affairs in this context. In the final analysis, group selling was neither feasible, popular, nor profitable.

Escaping from the stifling confines of the study neighborhood became the overriding objective. Sellers used a number of tactics to achieve "separation from the crowd." The simplest method was to be out early and stay out late, monopolizing sales during inconvenient time slots. Though MacCoun and Reuter contend that dealers who use such strategies "will frequently find themselves in conspicuous isolation (i.e., at high risk and with few income-generating opportunities),"[23] Skates and Fade felt otherwise:

Best time to sell in the mornin'. Six, seven a.m. Ain't got to worry about nothin' for real. No cats [rivals], no poh-lice trippin' on you. They [police] think you on your way to school. Ain't gonna trip on you.

I like sellin' late at night—three a.m.—ain't nobody out. The few car that do come through, they fixin' to spend some money. When you see a car hit the corner, you already know who it is. Only a buyer . . . come through that late.

Of course, off-peak selling was avoided by many sellers precisely because it *was* inconvenient and unlikely to result in significant rewards per unit of time expended. "Going the extra mile" contradicted the sellers' indolent orientation to life. Late-night, off-time sales also tend to attract the truly desperate crack fiend—one who probably is not able to spend a good deal of money or one who may ask for credit or try to pull a scam. Yet given the fierce competition and stagnating demand, stray sales become more important than ever. "Addicts geek here and there,"[24] and a few of these transactions a day for several days in a row can mean the difference between a great week and one significantly lacking in income. Not surprisingly, sellers seemed to recognize this and yet be loathe to act on it at the same time.

Being mobile was a more acceptable alternative. Mobility allowed offenders the latitude to move about when and where they wanted to, at times when a selling environment was likely to be target-rich. Mobility helped to attenuate the negative effects of declining demand and intense competition— providing flexibility to sellers who could troll for sales rather than remain at a fixed spot. As Deuce Low illustrated, "I get my rounds on 'round the hood. Half hour on Denny, half hour on Phillips, half hour on Joyner. I'm gettin' my rounds on. Catchin' a little somethin' [a sale] here and there." To be mobile was also to be elusive, essential in a context where being tied to a particular spot might draw the attention of patrolling police.

The more mobile the seller, however, the more likely he was to come on already established sellers. Though Pee Wee Dancer claimed, "If he on it, he on it. Everybody makin' money. It's all good," in reality, selling spots might or might not be honored. Spots once respected might devolve quickly into a chaotic, every-man-for-himself bum rush. The limited selling prospects contiguous to the study neighborhood only increased the likelihood of this. The study site was bounded on three sides by rival drug sets; venturing to these areas was risky. "It be all staticky [threatening] and shit around here," noted K-Rock.

Much of north St. Louis city is quilted by a patchwork of gang-affiliated drug sets, enmeshing gang and nongang curbside sellers and circumscribing their options. In general, sellers seldom cross into "foreign" areas—particularly those designated by gang boundaries. Such boundaries represent geographic as well as perceptual and psychological barriers to entry[25]—deflecting potential intruders by virtue of the socially constructed ownership particular groups have over a given parcel of land. Extraneighborhood mobility appeared to be limited to friendly constellations in other north-side areas. Affiliated sets claimed several sectors around the city, providing sellers (at least those with the means to travel to those sectors) a semblance of a social network to allow occasional expansion of their bleak selling prospects. As K-Rock remarked,

Maybe I just be drivin' 'round for a blow [driving while smoking marijuana] and need to make me a little money. I just go down to Teller and Denny. There's some Metros down there: "Who is you, blase, blase?" they say. "I'm OG four deuce, I know so and so, so and so, and so and so. Need to make a little grip for a little while. That cool?" Make a few sales and go on about my business.

There be Metros all 'round. Down on Garfield and Cleveland, Coolidge and Jackson, Lincoln and Ezra. Wherever [they are, I can sell]. I can sell all around 'cause there be nine-deuce, Metro Crips. I flash a sign, they flash me back, then I know what set they be claimin' [and if that set is friendly].

It was my sense, however, that such excursions were infrequent, spontaneous, and not available to the vast majority of sellers. It also was my sense that going to these sets might very well place dealers in the very selling conditions they sought to escape—high competition, limited demand, and indigent customers. The ability to move around the city itself, irrespective of gang affiliation, to sell for a few hours or days at a time in some specified location in which one had kin or friends, was preferable. As Blockett remarked,

The key is to not stay in one place very long. I be movin' all the time. . . . I'll go to North City, Central West, and North County. I'll stack my grip [make money] each place and then just do the cycle all over again.

Jimmy Hat claimed that every Saturday his brother would take him to the south side. He spoke highly of these sojourns, claiming that transactions there were for fifties and boppers, that "there a lot of white people over there [with considerably more money to spend], and that police ain't too hot." Jimmy Hat described his strong desire to focus his selling efforts on the south side only:

South side, ohhh man, I wish I could be there about seven days [a week]! They ain't comin' with no five, ten dollars over there. They comin' with twenty, twenty-five, thirty, fifty dollars. Money be comin' like this. I makes 'bout eight hundred fifty dollars [over a week] on the south side.

South St. Louis is a mix of white and black residents and exhibits much less of the acute social disorganization of the underclass north side study setting. With a few exceptions, south city may fairly be characterized as working class. Compared to the north, per capita income is generally higher, unemployment less chronic, social disorganization less severe, and crack users more "affluent." Any opportunity to go south and sell to consumers who were not dependent on public transfer payments was welcome. Only well-connected dealers, however—those with associates, friends, or kin in these locales—could truly be mobile. By and large, the offenders in my sample lacked the necessary resources to move about, reinforcing the isolated nature of their selling position and compelling them to resort to more proximal strategies to obtain sales. Cultivation was just such a strategy.

CULTIVATION

Sellers somehow had to differentiate an undifferentiated product, setting it apart from products of a multitude of other sellers within and without the neighborhood. Developing an inelastic demand with one or more customers can shield a given seller from withering competition. This requires a series of specific cultivation techniques. Cultivation techniques are "courting and wooing activities engaged in by servicers in relations with those whom they service." They "are employed with the intent of either directly or indirectly gaining a reward (usually monetary)."[26] Through such techniques, sellers can increase the amount of control they exercise in relationships with particular buyers over time. Control over buyers, in turn, gives them control over other sellers within and without the neighborhood with whom they are in competition: customers will seek out sellers who have "done them right."

The crucial importance of "loyalty-invoking behavior" has been noted in a wide variety of contexts—licit and illicit, economic and noneconomic.[27] In retail enterprise, repeat customers represent the backbone of most successful businesses. Regular customers are valued not only for their repeat purchasing, their predictability, and their familiarity but also as a possible source of new referrals. Insofar as sellers are concerned with the maintenance of working relations with a given set of customers, buyers may also be more likely to define the drugs they buy and the experience of buying within the context of these relations. In effect, to the extent that buyers perceive sellers to be effective "partners-in-trade," sellers may enjoy both greater immediate rewards and longer-term stability.[28]

In the world of illicit street drugs, the mythic importance of a good connection cannot be overstated. Most people involved in the generic process of purchasing want the most and best product for the least amount of money, and crack buyers evaluate dealers by seeking out those who are perceived to offer the best deal.[29] This is especially true of the street fiends these sellers modally served, who tend to treat every transaction as an extensive and irretrievable investment.[30] Unlike "normal" consumers, who tend to act in closer accordance with rational principles of supply, demand, value, and comparative shopping, hard-core crack users typically want to score as much as they can as fast as they can. Quite often, they have neither the time nor inclination to "shop around." Information about who has what, where it is, and how much it costs is therefore a "high-ranking need" that is not easily met, since street-level crack markets are in a constant state of flux.[31] Users' rationality is severely bounded, and they dislike tracking down alternative suppliers. Instead, buyers typically hedge their bets and seek the services of somebody with a proven track record.[32]

A number of sellers attempted to target their market strategies accordingly. Selling the fattest stones, offering more product for the money than was customary, and giving credit were all geared to entice customers to seek them and them only:

The bigger ones [rocks] you serve, the more customers you get. You don't gotta worry about no one else gettin' the sale because they [users] want you. (Bo Joe)

You give 'em more than what you should because they look at their's competitors and know that ain't what so and so gave me [last time]. (Ice-D)

Everybody try to keep they own clientele. Homie spoiled a customer so much last night, he don't wanta deal with me—only him. (Deuce Low)

Providing fat stones may hook customers into buying from a particular seller, but smaller quantities—provided sometimes at reduced cost or free of charge—keeps the addiction going. Cultivation is arguably most effective—and most appreciated—when users are at their height of desperation. In the twilight of a binge, for example, even the most meager form of generosity can look colossal and reflect positively on the dealer who is "compassionate" enough to offer a free or cut-rate nugget:

When a customer's geekin' . . . I'll break off some pieces, like give 'em a fifteen for ten, or a ten for five, or just break off like two- and three-dollar pieces to someone who ain't got nothin' right now. . . . I kinda feel guilty—know they got kids. So I don't be taxin' like that. You're gonna lose money, but you're gonna keep your clientele. You know they get paid at the first of the month, and they gonna keep spendin' with me [because I did that for them]. I'm true to the smokers. . . . That why my clientele be so high [numerous]. (K-Rock)

Offering credit was a second important aspect of customer cultivation. In the world of street crack, credit is traditionally arranged only among sellers. As Skolnick notes, "Similar trust is rarely extended to street customers. . . . This is sometimes attributable to the lack of personal knowledge of the buyer, which precludes the building of the necessary trust, and sometimes to the simple fact that the buyer is a cocaine user and as such is perceived to be unreliable."[33] Where the supply of dealers and demand for the substance they purvey is asymmetrical, however, an aggregate power imbalance will result and benefit those who are fewest in number. Clearly, buyers have the upper hand in a declining market, so sellers have to deploy whatever "leveling mechanisms" they can to try to balance things out.[34]

Extending the right amount of credit at the right time can forge brand loyalty and be profitable at the same time. Several sellers reportedly timed their offerings to coincide with the last week of the month, so that memories would be fresh when money became abundant the following week. "Yeah, I give credit like around the first—if you know them and know they'll come back. When they get they [public transfer] money, they gonna come back and spend it with me," explained Benzo. This could mean a real windfall, particularly if customers made their repayment along with an additional (and perhaps quite large) purchase. Other sellers extended credit to customers who had previously demonstrated enough financial wherewithal to be considered good risks—typically customers with regular jobs, steady access to cash (for example, from petty hustles), or both. As Bo Joe remarked:

Give somethin' on credit, ten or twenty dollars, and when they get they check, they pay you back. When more money comin' in [when customers come into more cash], they keep comin' to me.

Interest rates varied by the offender and were usurious to say the least—from the more forgiving sum of $5 a day on a $20 rock to a mafia-esque 100 percent rate—regardless of the amount involved—to be paid the following day or week. To an outsider, such arrangements seem foolish, but to thirsty crack users they make perfect sense. No matter how exorbitant the interest, those caught in the throes of an all-consuming addiction, without sufficient funds to continue using, may view getting crack on credit tantamount to getting crack free. Immediate gratification is essential and can occur at the expense of rational economic thinking.

To be sure, such arrangements may not be as sweet for dealers as they appear either. Although Fade emphasized the importance of extending credit only to "specific people that won't play with your money," the objective conditions he and others faced mitigated against prompt repayment. Delinquent customers often were difficult to find or, if found, unable to pay. Those most able to pay—by virtue of greater income, social capital, or control over their use—also were most likely to have alternative sources of supply and an effective means of evading repayment. Of course, the less credit dealers offered, the less they had to worry about coming up short or tracking down debtors. Yet the less credit dealers extended, the more restricted their sales and the more limited their customer base would be. As desperation mounts, sellers increase their risk of entering into shaky arrangements, in the misguided belief they will be paid back. The more interest they charge to make up for shortfalls, the less likely customers will be able to pay, and the more incentive there will be for debtors not to return. Arrangements intended to create inelastic demand in declining markets may have the opposite effect, resulting in the further erosion of one's client base.

In the final analysis, cultivation tactics—whether in the form of credit offerings, fat stones, or donation nuggets—clearly were not used because buyers were a "valued, long-term resource, whose favor and custom should be curried." [35] A kind of pseudofriendship guided such tactics, illustrated by the rather common expressions of "showing love" and "bless-

ing" customers that dealers associated with their benefi-
cent acts—even though the very tactics designed to make
crack demand more inelastic helped perpetuate their customers' pharmacological enslavement. Such is the world of illicit street drug sales, where friendship is sometimes measured by how generous one is in wreaking destruction on
another only too willing to accept it. That the majority of sellers voiced some guilt about their behavior is ironic but not remarkable. Their guilt was not necessarily heartfelt, and even
if it was, market conditions and the hard reality of need-
ing fast cash quickly overrode it. Double-D Loc, for example,
claimed that he was often tempted to take his stash and throw
it away out of guilt but never did so because, in his words, "If
I don't sell to them, they'll just go right over to someone else,
and they will make the money. It might as well be me." Skates
agreed:

I be sellin' that, it like killin' my brothers and sisters. It hurt my
feelin's when I gets to thinkin' about it. It make me wanna go flush
all my shit down the toilet. But if I do, I don't feel right 'cause they
just go out and get more from somewhere else.

Glenn Walters refers to such sentiments as *mollification*, a
process by which offenders attempt to "assuage, exonerate, or
extenuate responsibility for . . . [their] activities by pointing
out external considerations, which may or may not be true,
but which have nothing to do with [their] own behavior." [36]
The point is that even if one seller decided to forgo a particular cultivation episode, a host of others against whom they
measured their status would step in to fill the void. Occupational ambivalence is common among those who deal in tarnished goods and "dirty" people. [37]

CONCLUSION

Some commentators have speculated that drug dealing is a
good substitute for formal business training. It instills entrepreneurial skills and socializes young participants into the art

of customer relations, inventory, and cash-flow management. Neophyte capitalists learn to succeed in an unstable, competitive, and resource-scarce environment. To be successful, however, one must infuse a certain degree of rationality into one's operations. This often means forming hierarchical organizations and becoming functionally interdependent. For those accustomed to the rhythm and freedom of street life, organization and hierarchy are untenable propositions.[38]

As freelancers, the offenders in my sample are individual functionaries operating without any meaningful organizational template, cohesive exchange structure, or interdependent flow of tasks. Cooperative forms of selling are short-lived, infrequently observed, and generally limited to respecting each other's selling spot. Groups that emerged reflected a decentralized distribution system rather than a "coherent, formal, or lasting organization."[39] Plans to expand market share characteristically were parasitic and limited to individual sellers becoming more attentive about getting sales that came through or being better about stealing customers from others.

Ironically, it was these sellers' collective orientation and its provision of a definable, exclusive, "protected" turf on which to sell that played the pivotal role in shaping their group selling forms. Traditionally, protected markets are thought to be advantageous—particularly for gang-affiliated freelancers—by limiting competition that might otherwise undermine profits. Members can sell drugs in their own neighborhood without encroaching on the turf of others and can bar others from selling since this "territorial monopoly" is backed by force.[40] Gang affiliation also is said to "thwart the possibility of rip offs from would-be customers and robberies by rival gangs," to provide "lookouts to warn of police presence," and to offer a "measure of anonymity when police try to identify individual [sellers]."[41] The street gang is claimed to be an effective facilitator of drug sales because the collectivism it engenders complements the business side of dope selling.[42]

A second look reveals such benefits to be superficial at best. Although collective identification provides a modicum of protection, the territoriality that goes with it ensures that a significant number of sellers will be vying for a finite number of sales in a limited geographic frame. Protected markets keep outsiders out, but they keep affiliated participants in. The chaotic, predatory, and parasitic group selling arrangements that I found are not surprising and become particularly troublesome in a declining streetcorner market. Since the amount of money any given seller can make is finite (and reportedly smaller compared to years gone by), maximizing one's own sales at the expense of others becomes even more important.

Whether, when, and how intensely competition is likely to develop hinges on a number of factors. Surging prices serve as a signal for dealer entry.[43] Rising demand at certain times of the day, days of the week, or weeks of the month (for example, Thursday evenings, weekends, near the first) makes it easier or more profitable to sell at that time than at others and will attract a greater number of dealers. As dealer-to-customer ratios rise, market organization tends to destabilize, and sellers are more likely to rush to cars and passers-through in an attempt to steal sales from other dealers. With multiple persons vying for a finite but significant amount of cash, sellers also may be more likely to take risks about whom they sell to and generally may be more indiscreet in how they go about their business. Low-volume sales periods need not change things all that much. The more diffused a restricted number of sales are, the more desperate sellers are likely to become, and the more predatory their selling arrangements may be, at least in the short term. An alternative argument could be made that the promise of lower profits may actually check competition—assuming that the attractiveness of crack selling decreases in direct proportion to the allure of more convenient, available, or profitable substitutes. Sellers, for example, may choose to "lie low" and live off their savings until the volume of sales restabilizes, sell other substances (such as marijuana or heroin), or displace criminal activity to predatory, income-generating offenses.

The nature and degree of law enforcement also are likely to

influence emergent selling forms. Very intense, visible police initiatives tend to temper competition, and this can have a profoundly stabilizing effect on market organization.[44] Yet sellers do adapt. Windows of opportunity inevitably will be available, and pent-up transactional activity might be moved to these times. Indeed, it is conceivable that microbursts of selling activity can be sandwiched between even the most intense of crackdown periods. Undercover surveillance and selectively targeted, small-scale buy-and-bust tactics are unlikely to have the same kind of short-term effect. As learning curves come into play, however, increasing discretion on the part of sellers is more likely. The use of surveillance and other covert measures may actually have a more stabilizing effect on market organization over time than uniformed initiatives. When offenders never know if or when they are being watched, a kind of global discretion may be triggered through a panopticon effect: "I might be watched right now, so I better be careful about how I offend, or I'll be caught and punished." These and other issues relevant to social organization and social control are revisited in chapters 5 and 6.

Cultivating a brand-loyal cadre of personal customers becomes the most logical and effective response for sellers in the face of current market conditions. No matter how predatory conditions may become, the more a seller is able to distinguish his product from that of the crowd, the more likely he is to have a chance at selling discreetly. Of course, doing the things necessary to establish inelastic demand—giving bigger rocks for the money, offering lenient credit arrangements, or providing rocks for free in times of user desperation—undermine a seller's fiscal footing and his ability to continue selling, especially in a declining streetcorner market where there is little margin for cultivation. Other sellers also can adopt the same tactics, neutralizing those who initiate them first, leveling the playing field, and making everyone worse off.[45] The inferior product that streetcorner sellers generally have to purvey—drugs become progressively diluted as they move downward through the dealing chain—may make their product "uncultivatable" to begin with. In addition, the increased investment of time required to cultivate carries with it more potential risk. Street crack users, in this regard, are often perceived to be the most vexing of customers to deal with—owing largely to their chronic dependence and desperation to make the best deal possible. "They try to be choicy," A-Train complained. "Takin' all day, tryin' to be foolin' around, tryin' to get over, [and in the meanwhile] police gonna swoop." Yet sellers could not dismiss the importance of cultivating brand loyalty or ignore the fact that this cultivation might require extended time spent together completing a transaction. As demand continues to stagnate and buyer-seller relations become increasingly asymmetrical, the short-term outlook for curbside vendors is likely only to worsen.

4 Predators

There are few settings more anomic than the streetcorner drug market. Burns, ripoffs, and violence are everyday occurrences in a world that is systematically organized around predation and mutual exploitation. It is a "crime attractor" in the true sense of the term, a context that offers "easy, safe, and profitable" criminal opportunities to motivated offenders bent on victimizing others.[1] The epidemic levels of assault, theft, and homicide experienced between 1984 and 1991 were fueled primarily by crack's emergence onto the street scene.[2] Psychopharmacological, economically compulsive, and systemic factors[3] were all causally implicated. Crack alters mood in users, resulting in increased excitability, irrationality, and aggressiveness. Smoking crack rapidly becomes costly, impelling users to commit income-generating crimes to sustain their habits. Predation and violence, finally, are intrinsic to crack market participation. These stem from conflicts over money, quality, and territory.

The crack crime wave was arguably the worst of any drug epidemic. At the zenith of its popularity, significantly more persons used and sold the drug than ever used or sold heroin or cocaine powder (at the height of these respective drug eras). Large numbers of crack market participants were heavy daily consumers, using the substance in unparalleled amounts and frequencies.[4] Since the crack high lasts only a short time, creates a compulsive need for more, and inevitably results in a postuse crash, key pharmacological triggers were in place to foment behavioral instability. Moreover, crack market participants typically engaged in transactions in ways that elevated their "personal and aggregate risk" (such as impulsive buying and selling habits, multiple supply sources, and large and unregulated dealing networks).[5] Coupled with the explosion of firearm availability that coincided with crack's emergence, the widespread arming of drug market participants, the casual way in which many participants used these weapons, and the diffusion of guns to persons peripherally involved in the scene, it is not surprising that the street crack landscape came to resemble something out of the Wild West.

With crack's decline came social stabilization. Relative to the chaotic days of the late 1980s and early 1990s, many users and dealers in the middle to late 1990s began conducting business in a more controlled manner. The need to recruit large numbers of young sellers—the demographic segment most responsible for lethal violence—lessened. Combined with increasing community involvement in dispute arbitration, greater job availability in a rapidly growing economy, and incapacitation effects from swelling prison populations, street crack markets stabilized.[6] But systemic, economically compulsive, and psychopharmacological factors continued to exert a defining influence. This chapter explores the persisting climate of threat in a stagnating curbside market and examines the form and content of dangers, sellers' responses to them, and the way such responses may facilitate the very outcomes sellers seek to avoid.

GETTING OVER

A crack habit is expensive, and the ability to generate money legitimately declines as addiction progresses. "Hustling" emerges as a primary method of sustaining use. To be "on the hustle" is to engage in unconventional activities for the purpose of economic or narcotic gain. "Getting over"—the conduct norm that drives the process—is one of the strongest of drug market behavioral prescriptions, regardless of the substance involved or the historical era. Its importance is especially pronounced for hard-core, street-level crack users— given their compulsive use and advanced stage of addiction. What such users may lack in capital they can make up for in skill, a cultivated skill that, for some, becomes something of a fine art. Those able to "get over" consistently earn an elevated status of sorts—"expressed on a daily basis in intimate and public constructions of self-respect."[7]

On one end of the predation continuum, sellers confront a steady and predictable barrage of users who are trying in some form or fashion to take them in. The most innocuous of such attempts involves pleas for more crack than users are willing or able to pay for. Such overtures fall under the "'It's worth a try' genre'"[8] and are not unlike the attempts of young children to cajole their parents into springing for a cheap toy at an amusement arcade. As Agar (1973) notes, expectations of success are low, but the potential payoff is sufficiently high to justify the effort. Dealers reported these pleas to be linked either to proclamations of affection or to allegations that the quantity or quality of the stones offered was inadequate:

They try to get fifty for fifteen, or somethin' like that, sayin', "Show me some love, show me some love. We peoples, we peoples [family]." (Benzo)

They try to tell you your stones don't taste right or they too small, but they be shysty. They [just use that] to tell me to "show 'em some love." (Tony Mack)

Sellers have to gauge whether a customer truly is desperate or is simply trying to snooker them. Entreaties also could not be considered outside the context of specific exchange relationships and dealers' competitive pursuit of brand loyalty. Cultivation and exploitation are flip sides of the same coin, how-

ever, and this opens up a source of vulnerability for dealers. One might give a rock to a begging user only to find out
that the person had spent a considerable sum of money with
someone else shortly thereafter. Or a seller might give credit
when none was needed—convinced by a duplicitous customer who had no intention of repayment.

Unwarranted customer cultivation was anathema. It identified the seller as a "mark," a reputation that is anything but
good on the streets, especially in a declining market. Sellers
were vulnerable on several fronts: because a host of sellers
within and without the immediate area was available to serve
a given customer, because brand loyalty was so important,
because particular sellers did not have detailed knowledge of
every user's buying history, and because sellers may have
been overconfident about their ability to avoid "getting
beaten." Wily customers could search for susceptible targets
in multiple sets, exploit one or more, and be reasonably confident that they wouldn't be recognized or tracked down. Sellers sought to minimize the number of times this happened,
being skeptical yet retaining a posture for cultivation.

The furtive nature of the street crack sale confounds this
imperative and makes a seller's fleecing, in some cases, virtually undetectable. Typically, the schemes employed to do this
rely on sleight of hand, counterfeiting, or crude con games.
Plagued by the gnawing fear of being robbed, arrested, or having a sale stolen by another dealer, a seller's mental attention
might be diverted just enough for a buyer to filch a "windfall"
without the seller noticing until it is too late. Each scam,
therefore, was structured to use the seller's need for a rapid
hand-to-hand transaction against him. Skates recounted a
sleight-of-hand maneuver pulled on him—made possible by
the window of opportunity he provided:

Dude came to me and wanted a fifty. I saw the two twenties and
a ten he was showed. I went to get the rock [from a stash spot, to
minimize the quantity of on-person crack he would have if robbed
or arrested], and he gave me the money, all folded up. He rode off,
but it was only a twenty and a ten, not [the] two twenties and a ten

he had showed me. It looked like a whole fifty [when he had folded it up and given it to him], but it was only thirty.

The use of counterfeit money capitalized on similar dynamics. Furtive hand-to-hand street exchanges make verification of the number of bills and their denomination difficult—especially at night. Verification is confounded further by the "kind" of money street crack customers might bring to transactions—dirty, crumpled, balled up, torn, or otherwise damaged dollar bills. This crumpled mass of currency provides a "sharp hook"[9] for money-hungry sellers and offers buyers the opportunity to configure small-denomination bills around specially cut pieces of regular paper (made to resemble a large wad of cash). In some sense, "clucker money," as dealers refer to it, was comforting because no undercover cop was perceived to be despairing or dramaturgically skilled enough to make their buy money look this way. For many street crack users, currency deterioration happens as a matter of course. Double-D Loc was defrauded in this fashion:

Dude asked to buy a twenty. I gave him the stone and got the money, but by the time I count it, it was fake and he was gone. It was like a five-dollar bill wrapped around pieces of newspaper.

One of the more ingenious petty scams reported was a contemporary version of a tried-and-true confidence game. Confidence games are plots where confederates gain the trust of a "mark" and convince him that he will receive the good or service for which he is about to pay. In reality, the con has no intention of meeting his end of the bargain.[10] A crack user, for example, might change orders from small to large and back to small in quick succession, giving increments of cash along the way, confusing sellers, and baiting them into giving a larger amount than he or she paid for. Ice-D found it difficult to put into words what had happened to him—attesting to the scheme's effectiveness:

Old man [customer] came and wanted fifteen for ten. Take it out my hand, and he just gimme five. I broke off a piece of a twenty for

a five, then he wanted to see what else I had, and I gave him another piece, and then he said, "All I want is a five," and [he] gave
back more of what I had gave him. He gave me a five [dollar bill],
but he got nearly a twenty [by switching everything around and
confusing me]. It's funny. I can barely explain right now. I even
told my partners, and they couldn't understand.

With experience, sellers wise up to these and other petty
schemes, making their success fleeting. The learning curve is
perhaps longer for less experienced sellers, but they too identify the form and content and learn how not to be taken. Getting burned by drive-through customers who "smash off"
with the merchandise, by contrast, was less defensible because
it occurred without any transactional foreplay, as it were.

Drive-through service is a marketing innovation developed during the crack epidemic's expansion phase.[11] Its intent
is to increase the volume of available customers, increase the
frequency of sales (since customers with cars will tend to have
greater financial resources and thus are more likely to return
for additional drugs), facilitate the flow of customers through
a selling area, and attract buyers from distant locales where
crack may have been unavailable. Intentions aside, drive-
through sales increase sellers' vulnerability in a number of
ways. Protected by locked doors and shatter-resistant windows, buyers can exploit a clear power asymmetry in the spatial proxemics of the exchange. Buyers are able to control
their exposure—by raising and lowering windows and brak-
ing and accelerating as they choose. Buyers also can conceal
and produce firearms with ease, placing sellers in a real
quandary, particularly those rushing headlong to get a sale.

The dynamics of armed victimizations and the problems
they present for sellers are detailed below (in "Armed Victimization"). The modal form of drive-through burn was
nonviolent but no less impoverishing: customers sped away
with rocks dropped in their hand by careless sellers who failed
to secure payment first. "I gave it [the rock] to him [a drive-
up customer]," Ice-D recounted, "and he play like he was
gonna gimme the money—reachin' all in his pockets and

everything. Then he just smashed off." Skates insisted that he doesn't "do that no more. Now you gimme the money off the top before I give 'em anything." Bump and runs were a variation on the same burn. In this scheme, a customer would pull to the curb, roll the car window down part or all the way, and ask to see the stones up close—not an unreasonable request given the desire to select the best rock. Once the seller's hand was inside the vehicle, however, the buyer would slyly reach underneath the hand, hit it upward to spill the rocks into the car, and speed off. As Double-D Loc recounted:

Dude drove up, I was gonna make the sale. So I go up to the window fixin' to serve him, my hand be out [and cupped] to give him a rock, and he just knocked my hand up and drove off. I had eight twenties [and lost them all].

Short Dog discussed a collective version of the same type of scam, where he and three of his dealing partners had bum rushed a customer's car with outstretched palms, chock full of rocks. The customer coolly allowed each of their rock-bearing hands to enter the passenger compartment, ostensibly to inspect the merchandise. Then in one sudden motion, he jarred all their hands upward—dumping the booty in the car—and peeled off.

There was essentially no way to retrieve rocks lost in this fashion. Clutching desperately for the customer or the ignition keys, punching the window, or chasing the car as it screeched away were knee-jerk reactions and typically done in vain. Sellers rarely had firearms on their person—a response to aggressive stop, search, and frisk procedures instituted by the St. Louis Police Department. Since immediate retribution was unlikely, sellers claimed to have adopted a number of policies to prevent such burns. One was to require customers to turn off the ignition and remove the keys before a sale. As Deuce Low explained, "I make 'em cut the car off first. They might be so geeked up they try to pull off with the shit. They be 'noid [paranoid] with us, so we gotta be 'noid with them." Another tactic was for the seller to cup his palm tightly enough so that rocks could not spill out, even if the hand was bumped violently. Other tactics involved spitting a rock into one's hand and clutching it tightly only after a specific request for a particular-size stone, refusing to place rock-containing palms too close to car windows, approaching the passenger's side rather than the driver's side to create spatial distance between the driver-user (making bump and runs virtually impossible), requiring customers to open the window all the way to prevent the seller from having to put his hands inside the vehicle, requiring customers to exit the vehicle to conduct the sale face to face, and ordering customers to allow entry into the vehicle while carrying out the sale as buyer and seller drive around the block.

The extent to which sellers actually used such practices was mediated by any number of situational factors. Fierce competition, saturation patrol, exchange relationships with specific customers, or excessive impulsivity on the part of any given seller all could work against circumspection. Of course, dropping one's guard, even for a moment, is long enough to be taken. On the streets there is no second chance, and one must always be at a full state of alert. Trust is a precarious and evanescent quality and may lead to assumptions about behavior that are discordant with reality. "Trusted customers" one moment can become exploitive antagonists the next. This is particularly true of hard-core street crack users—arguably the most unstable, volatile, and greediest of all drug consumers. With them, caution and prudence on the part of sellers are most important, yet both may be most vulnerable to suspension given the desperation for sales and thirst for profit in a stagnating streetcorner market.

THE DILEMMA OF STREET EXCHANGES

Although sellers underscore the importance of not giving up rocks without getting their money first, buyers were equally concerned about getting the rocks before giving up their money. Street drug dealers routinely exploit their customers—by tapping bags, substituting inert compounds, shortchanging, or taking off with the cash.[12] Buyers had no assurance that they would not receive a fake or undersized rock as sellers disappeared behind tenements, down gangways, or into vacant lots.

Presale testing therefore is essential for buyers. Although visual inspection offers some indication of product quality, users must learn to taste a small amount and judge from physical sensations whether it is good dope. But the furtive nature of the street sale does not lend itself to examining or verifying the most elementary aspects of the sale. This renders even the crudest of tests difficult.[13] The highly charged transactional moment—in which both parties' attention is consumed with the business at hand and also with the fear of being victimized or apprehended—is disconcerting and reinforces the perceived need to complete the sale quickly. The cruel paradox is that the speedier the transaction, the more furtive it becomes, and the less control one can exercise over its outcome. Delays are inevitable as cat-and-mouse games are played in which each party orders the other to hand over the goods. Each is reticent to budge—the seller worried that the buyer will take off with the merchandise and the buyer worried that the seller will take the money and run or hand over a fake or undersized rock. The whole scene can be seen as resembling a huge game of chicken: whoever gives in first will have committed irrevocably to a course of action that they no longer control. Though the financial stakes involved on the streetcorner generally are small, they are acute and irretrievable, and one can lose what might have taken significant time or effort to accumulate. In the end, both buyer and seller may be so oblivious to anything but not getting fleeced that each ends up under arrest. Brand-loyal relations (for buyers) and shared social history (for sellers) moderate and mediate this process, but neither guarantees to expedite a given transaction given the persistent levels of mistrust, desperation, fear, and ambiguity.

For whatever it is worth, offenders claimed rarely to scam their customers. Doing so, sellers insist, risks both physical injury and loss of reputation. The veracity of their statements is questionable. As C. Wright Mills notes, "The differing reasons men give for their actions are not themselves without reasons."[14] Sellers may have wanted to appear righteous to themselves or to me, since drug selling is their primary source of "professional" status. In reality, burning customers often is necessary to maintain profitability in a business where profit margins are thin and getting thinner. The need to burn becomes particularly pressing following an arrest or confiscation of one's dope or money, on the heels of a wild spending spree, or during a citywide drought in supplies of cocaine—none of which are uncommon. Desperation can drive the most "upright" of sellers to burn a long-time customer—perhaps even one they had labored to cultivate. That sellers have something to gain financially from selling fake drugs (at least for a time) and little to fear juridically, makes it easier: if arrested for selling an "imitation controlled substance," sellers might spend a couple of days at most in jail and be released after laboratory results reveal the substance to be other than an illegal drug. Since the circuit attorney's office generally will not issue complaints on "imitation" cases (given the backlog of real drug cases), selling a couple of "fake twenties" might well be worth it.

A popular bogus concoction whipped up by offenders was a frozen blend of baking soda, candle wax, and Oragel—which produced oral numbing and mimicked the brittle consistency of crack. Almonds, candle wax, Velamints, and gravel—sealed in cellophane and made to look like real crack rocks—also were described. The packaging makes rocks look bigger than they are and difficult to test without opening them first—something sellers frown on and may prohibit out of their fear of detection or of getting burned themselves if drug buyers substitute a prefabricated, phony rock during the tasting process for the seller's real one. This "burn bag" will then be knowingly or unknowingly passed onto another customer.[15]

Burning customers is inherently self-limiting, though, and

typically effective for only a brief time. Once a customer is exploited like this, he or she is unlikely to return—except for revenge. Burning customers has collective repercussions as well. It gives the drug set a bad name and deters customers from coming back at the very time when customers are needed most. As destitution mounts, sellers become more prone to "rip and run"—triggering a cycle of reinforcing behavior that contributes to further demand stagnation. Collectively and individually, sellers ultimately may find themselves trapped in a "crab's dilemma, in which the desperate crabs at the bottom of the bucket grab the legs of those trying to climb out and pull them back down."[16]

ARMED VICTIMIZATION

Point-of-sale hustles and straight burns are the more innocuous ways by which sellers are separated from their valued contraband. More ominous and threatening are the armed robberies that victimize streetcorner crack dealers. Street crack dealers make particularly good robbery victims. They are out in the open, have ready cash, hold valuable and portable contraband, may be wearing expensive luxury items, and generally will not report the offense to the police. There is, after all, "no 911 for [street] criminals."[17] Even if a police report is made, authorities often write it off or remark that the dealer got what he deserved.[18] Observers are disinclined to intervene, and bystanders reluctant to come forward as witnesses: on the streets, the ability to mind one's own business is crucial to survival since snitching can have disastrous consequences. Not surprisingly, active St. Louis armed robbers liken victimizing streetcorner crack dealers to "taking stick candy from a baby."[19]

Though researchers have found that drug-selling groups with "more articulated structures" have been associated with higher levels of violence, violence and its threat are ubiquitous on the streets no matter what the degree of organization.

Moreover, violence can happen with little warning since surprise is a critical element in its use. Would-be offenders also are familiar with their intended targets and know where to find them, making an already unstable situation even more combustible.[20]

One of the most important prerequisites of any successful armed street robbery is to "fit into the social setting such that the intended victim perceives the would-be attacker's presence as normal and nonthreatening, thereby allowing them to get close enough for a surprise attack."[21] The apparent customer who becomes an actual robber presents street crack dealers with an unsolvable dilemma. The fluidity of the two roles offers robbers a strategic advantage by providing an accepted means of establishing copresence while concealing, or at least delaying, the exposure of their true intentions. As such, there is little opportunity for would-be victims to recognize the danger and mount some sort of preemptive strike.[22] Fade tells of a drive-up sale turned robbery:

> Dude came up to me, wanted a fifty. I'm ready to serve, and he be reachin' in his pocket, like he be reachin' for the money, then he pull out a damn .44 magnum on me! He told me to give 'em the dope. I'm like, "You playin', man," and he's like, "No, it's a real motherfuckin' gun. Gimme the dope, and move 'way from the motherfuckin' car!" I [did what he said], stepped back, and he pulled off.

Similarly, Skates described being approached by a vehicle containing what were ostensibly customers. Then three gunmen wearing ski masks jumped out and chased him down. Out of breath and broke, Skates boldly dared the disbelieving predators to "Kill me now, right on the spot" and declared that he "wasn't afraid to die over no robbery." After a thorough search turned up nothing, the gunmen reportedly meted out some mild physical punishment and left. Likewise, K-Rock was robbed of $700 in gold chains, pocket money, and his shoes. Reportedly, the robbers put the gun to his head and cocked it, whereupon he looked in their eyes and told them soberly, "'Do what you gotta do.' He [one of the robbers] look in my eyes, like he was scared or something. Then they broke [ran]." Having nothing of value to give a potential victimizer is a dangerous proposition, something street ethnographers try to avoid by carrying so-called mugging money to offer in the event they are robbed.[23]

Having others around is perhaps the best deterrent. The cheapest and most effective insurance policy, after all, is to surround oneself with persons who have the same to lose and fear.[24] Though the presence of multiple sellers in competitive pursuit of the same goal impairs sales and profits, collective enterprise—no matter how parasitic—can help thwart armed robberies by offering natural surveillance and strength in numbers. "You want someone with you," Bo Joe explained, "'cause you never know what somebody gonna try." As Deuce Low put it, "If somebody robbed, we gonna get together [and help that person retaliate]. Everybody got they own hustle, but when we gangbang, we gangbang together." "The set already be deep," Pee Wee Dancer explained. "If someone come through the set [who tries to pull something], we just start bangin' with 'em, rush 'em off the set." Fellow sellers also can serve as human shields in the event of a random or drive-by shooting. This is important to those especially hated and sought by rivals.[25]

The presence of peers does not necessarily make one safer, however. Copresence can attract the very attention that leads to being victimized. The environment in which offenders live and sell drugs is saturated with predators. This can create isomorphic conditions in which offenders and offender-victims are joined together in space and time.[26] That sellers call the streets "home" for extended periods of time throughout a given day—a response to overcrowded housing arrangements[27] and the need to be accessible to customers—increases the likelihood that such conditions will manifest themselves. Selling by oneself, out of secret "cuts" (such as gangways, basement pits, vacant lots, alleyways, and spaces behind or between buildings), is not necessarily safer. Predators might identify a seller's locus of operation, sneak up, and corner him with no escape. The more secure the cut, the less chance one has to flee as one seals the very fate he seeks to avoid. In the final analysis, sellers have to reconcile themselves to the fact that violent confrontations can occur at any time and perhaps in situations having nothing to do with selling drugs. As Jimmy Hat recounted:

We was up at the liquor store. Had some yack [crack] in my shoes, when some cats [predators] pulled up and said they got some bo [weed], do we want some? "Got bo right here," I said. I could tell somethin' up with 'em, though, just by how they said it and how they was actin'. Went inside [the liquor store] and came back out [apparently by himself], and they had driven back around and came up on me and said, "You all playin' and shit [selling crack]. Give it up!" and he put his gun on me. I reach in my pocket, but I only give him half the money I had in there. Then he reach in there and get the rest. Then I drop my watch on purpose before I hand it to him, just to fuck with him. "I outta shoot you!" he said. Then he told me to take off my shoes and hand 'em over, but his partner said, "No, fuck that." See, I had that crack in my shoes, but they never got that. They took my shit and burned out.

Short Dog and Deuce Low, wearing gold, reported walking down to a nearby restaurant with some other sellers when armed offenders stormed into the restaurant, held them up, and took their possessions. Double-D Loc claimed to have been robbed twice with a gun, once for a $400 Turkish (gold chain), another for $900 in rings and a $100 beeper. On one of these occasions, he was playing basketball and "flashing" these items so that "people gonna peep it if they walk by and see me," at which point two robbers "stuck him up." "I put my golds in my mouth now," he explained matter-of-factly. Though some may have believed themselves secure by wearing valuables only at certain times or places, such a strategy is misguided. In a circumscribed social world teeming with predators, the threat of robbery is omnipresent. No sellers commented on the irony of being put at greatest risk of being robbed by the very items they purchased to proclaim their status as money-making street entrepreneurs.

RETRIBUTION?

In general, crimes against other criminals—crack sellers or not—are decidedly risky. Fellow criminals are more likely than regular citizens "to resist hold-up efforts and to seek out the perpetrator of [thefts]." Violence and, more important, the threat of it through retaliation are instrumental in maintaining order on the streets, where blood cancels all debts.[28] Robbing a curbside crack seller is by no means a risk-free proposition.

Though offenders waxed ferocious about what they would do if and when they were victimized, their bark appeared to be worse than their bite. Only one case of a planned and successful retaliation was reported, and this occurred only because the perpetrators remained in the immediate vicinity to inspect their booty before departing:

> They [the robbers] just stayed [in their car] over on Corson [a nearby street], lookin' at the [gold] chains [they had just stolen]. My homie got his double-barrel twelve-gauge [from a nearby dwelling], and he just came up behind them; they was sittin' there with the door open, so the light be on. They try to pull away, but my partner shot [into the back window] seven times [and then we ran]. Heard sirens. (K-Rock)

For the more innocuous scams and burns discussed earlier, the extent to which sellers could or did seek revenge was limited. Tracking down petty brigands not only is difficult, but it takes time, foresight, and planning—qualities few offenders can muster. Given their desperation for customers, the availability of the same undifferentiated product in nearby locales, and the general state of stagnating demand, a certain sense of ambivalence seemed to prevail about punishing customers they did track down—or punishing them as swiftly or as severely as they may have in days gone by. As Skates put it, now "we don't kill him, just whoop him."

The offenders' tough talk and posture for retribution may be just that—talk and posturing. The "don't mess with me," "crazy" reputation is said to provide street crack sellers a measure of inoculation from victimization.[29] Bourgois calls it a "personal logic of violence in the streets' overarching culture of terror," where the real or quasi-real threat of retaliation intimidates would-be offenders.[30] However interpreted, it speaks to the importance of fearlessness and "true nerve" as venerated character traits on the streets.[31] As anyone who has ever been in a schoolyard fight can tell you, backing down from a bully only promises to make future confrontations more likely. The reality of the situation, however, seems to be that street crack dealers lack the "organized intelligence and muscle necessary to exact retribution," dismiss scams and stick-ups as an "occupational hazard," and accept their losses with "equanimity."[32]

CONCLUSION

The extent to which victimization and its threat restrict the growth, expansion, or existence of streetcorner crack markets is an issue that cries for more systematic attention.[33] Whether streetcorner crack sellers "deserve" their victimization—considering the personal and societal destruction they wreak by selling their product—is a separate and hotly contested issue. It is safe to say, however, that no crack dealer will stay in business, or will stay in business for long, if he allows himself to be victimized.[34] Unfortunately for sellers, victimization is part of doing business. Their accessibility, the furtive transactional atmosphere, and the lack of formalized protocol for hand-to-hand exchanges institutionalize it, while the lack of legal recourse works against its remedy. This becomes particularly distressful for curbside sellers in declining markets and is likely to become more acute in the near term.

As demand stagnates, dealer-to-customer ratios tend to increase. To the extent that the need for furtiveness and transactional brevity rises—to avoid unwanted scrutiny from concerned citizens, armed predators, and police—indiscreet selling forms will become more prevalent. Windows of time previously available to "regulate" transactions consequently dissipate or fail to develop. Sellers in stagnating markets also may become more prone to suspending certain transaction-securing protocols—such as getting closer to customers or handling product for sale in less prudent ways—to which they may have otherwise adhered. Moreover, mental lapses almost inevitably occur in the heated battle of trying to beat out multiple others for a sale, and those lapses bring attendant dangers for sellers.

Brand-loyal relations between particular exchange parties—a strategic imperative for sellers in declining markets—would, at first glance, seem to modify these outcomes. On closer examination, however, it may actually do the opposite, at least in the short term: the perceived sense of security associated with brand-loyal relations may cause certain sellers to feel "safe" when they should not and lead them to suspend transaction-securing protocols they otherwise may have enacted. Given that power asymmetries benefiting buyers in declining markets make brand loyalty more tenuous than sellers think it to be, such a scenario is well within the realm of possibility.

Furtive transactions are not completely disadvantageous, of course. The omnipresent threat of arrest and severity of legal sanctions mandate that hand-to-hand street exchanges be done as quickly as possible. Transactional duration and detection risk are directly correlated; the quicker the transaction, the less fear one has of being detected. Yet this too may have negative consequences. Sellers, for example, may be enticed into keeping more rocks on their person rather than hidden in some secret spot nearby: the potential sales lost in time spent hustling to and from a stash spot is an opportunity cost few are in a position to bear. Ultimately, this may elevate the magnitude and seriousness of a fleecing incident. Boom periods of demand (such as near the first week of the month), where the dealer-to-customer ratio moderates, would not seem to change things altogether. Competition is likely to become even more intense since there's more money to be made, the amount is finite and zero-sum, and the time to make it is limited. Sellers may be more likely to keep large quantities of drugs on them to service the demand, increasing their vulnerability both to stick-up artists and to police who might appear at any moment, catching them with larger, more sanctionable quantities.

Even if stashing does not negatively affect sales frequencies (for example, when demand is completely inelastic), it may not necessarily be the wisest course of action. A number of sellers reported that their peers would steal their stash if the opportunity presented itself. "If they [fellow sellers] find out where it is, you best believe you won't have your shit no more," K-Rock explained. "Shit, yeah. They take it!" Double-D Loc agreed. "Somethin' I really don't understand." Deuce Low claimed that his "partners" were "shysty and ondry [scheming]," while K-Rock concluded derisively that they would "fuck your girl, rape your daughter, try to rob you, kill you, over one little bitty misunderstanding." Though stashes by and large are within sight of their owner, they might be left temporarily unsupervised for any number of reasons, such as after a seller is arrested on an outstanding warrant or when a seller is inattentive while drinking, talking, or shooting dice. A number of sellers stressed the importance of preventing the identification of stash spots by traveling to them sparingly, at odd times, or in circuitous routes. As Deuce Low explained, "I walk past my stash spot, go all the way around, hit a gangway, hit a little cut, come back round the block, and go to the stash spot. They [other sellers] probably think I comin' from a cut, a little chill spot, or somethin'." Double-D Loc subdivided his stash, hiding it in four separate spots to hedge against losing it all. Other sellers reported going to stashes only very early in the morning or late at night to avoid being seen and having their route traced.

Stash stealing and the procedures followed to prevent it clearly are not associated with those who hold their colleagues in high regard. An undeniable ambivalence can be heard in the sentiments of gang-affiliated street dealers, who speak of tightly bonded social relationships with fellow sellers and yet demonstrate an utter lack of trust and solidarity through the burns they pull on each other. Popular stereotypes of gang-affiliated crack slingers as family members whose bonds of kinship deter them from committing intentionally predatory behavior against one another are without a doubt off target. There was no collective conscience here in the classic Durkheimian sense, no shared value system that deterred within-group victimization.[35] The shared values that became most apparent were greed, mistrust, and mutual exploitation. Stealing another seller's stash when the opportunity presents itself is not only acceptable; it is justified. This is particularly true in a stagnating streetcorner market, where resources are increasingly scarce, and personal aspirations for wealth remain high.

5 Police

Of all illicit drug dealers, curbside crack sellers are the most vulnerable to police detection. Their activity is both "more noxious" and "more susceptible" to social control than that of any other type of dealer—more noxious because it is "obtrusive on the sensibilities of others" and more susceptible because open dealing can easily be observed and participants "provide ready targets for police search."[1] Initiatives to stop these offenders typically have focused on policies—stricter law enforcement and legislative stakes-raising—that enhance the deterrent power of sanctions.[2] Saturation patrol, neighborhood crackdowns, intensified surveillance, periodic drug sweeps, and stiff penalties attest to the extent to which resources are mobilized to "disrupt, dismantle, and ultimately destroy" these offenders.[3] Though such tactics thwart curbside crack sellers, they do not vanquish them. Evidence indicates that such strategies may be working but only marginally. There is little proof that they are superior to alternative, less draconian approaches: certainty of punishment, not severity, is foremost in sellers' minds, and many offenders continue to believe that they will never be caught. The tactics they adopt to ensure this outcome comprise the focus of this chapter.

HANDLING DRUGS AND
MANAGING ENVIRONMENTS

Wariness, monitoring, and fleet reactions to emergent threats are critical to actors in any strategic environment. But what may be routine for "normals" can become a grave management problem for those in serious violation of the law.[4] Social control agents can lurk anywhere in any number of forms—from patrol cars, unmarked or undercover vehicles rolling through an area, to surveillance officers parked secretly nearby documenting illegal activity. Offenders therefore have to (1) minimize the probability of being caught with drugs on their person and (2) minimize the probability of having significant quantities on them if they are caught.

Sellers interviewed in this study retained only small quantities of rocks on their person for immediate sale, cloistering larger inventories in some proximal place for "reupping" purposes. Typically, sellers concealed their on-person rocks orally and less frequently held them in their hands or pockets: police at close range could readily see evidence being held and dropped but could not readily detect caches hidden in a mouth. Sellers customarily had no more than two to five $20 rocks in their mouths at any point in time—less than a gram's worth. Two favorite hiding places were between the upper lip and upper gum and underneath the tongue. From here, rocks could be produced for sale quickly and without noticeable effort, providing ample opportunity to eliminate evidence (by swallowing it) if necessary and to retrieve it again when conditions were safe (by vomiting up rocks—packaged in cellophane wrap—after police retreated). Both hiding spots also minimized the appearance of protruding bulges, making rocks virtually undetectable to the naked eye. Indeed, I was amazed at the facility with which dealers conversed during interviews while they had as many as five $20 rocks in their mouths. A number of times, I didn't realize they were in there until later. The technique became so automatic for Blockett that he accidentally ate a rock while lunching. "I was pissed," he recounted. "That was twenty bucks."

Excess inventory—rocks needed for reupping purposes—
were stashed in, on, or immediately around their person. En-
vironmentally hidden stashes generally were placed not more
than several feet from their owner. They typically were in
line of sight but hidden in such a way as to (1) prevent discovery by police, fellow sellers, or voracious dope fiends and
(2) if discovered, particularly by the police, be unlinkable
to the seller who placed them there.[5] Typically, a stash would
be placed in such a way that only the particular seller who put
it there knew how to find it (at least theoretically). Each stash
had an individual "signature," but virtually all had a pro-
tective cellophane outer shell to protect rocks from the elements. Some stashes were swaddled in newspaper and buried
in dirt, with a uniquely shaped stick, mound of grass, piece
of candy, penny, bottle, or cigarette butt placed over the top
to mark it. Others were deposited in soda cans in Dumpsters,
on ledges in gangways, in hollowed-out sections of tree
trunks, or in bushes with tissue paper or newspaper draped
over them. The streets often are littered with the secret
stashes of individual dealers. "Right now, you could be sittin'
on top of a whole fuckin' pile of rocks," OG quipped as he observed me squatting on the ground, "and you wouldn't even
know it."

On-person stash spots for inventory (that is, rocks not for
immediate resale) include hollowed-out sticks dealers carry
with them, headbands of ball caps they wear, socks, or, for
dealers with "fros," their hair. One particularly confident
dealer used electrical duct tape to secure his stash under his
armpit. "Poh-lice never be checkin' there when they pat you
down," Blockett said as he replicated a typical police pat-down
on me. "They check your arms, sides, waist, legs, and ankles,
but poh-lice ain't never check *under* your arms." Baby Mayne
stashed his rocks between his toes. Apprehended once, he was
strip-searched and told to remove his shoes and socks. While
removing the latter, he reportedly allowed the stashed rocks
to slide from between his toes to under his feet. As he stood
up, he covered the rocks with the soles of his feet. Finding no
evidence, police allowed him to dress. He then reportedly

slipped the rocks back into his socks as he pulled them on, making a narrow escape.

Perhaps the favorite on-person spot for inventory not for immediate sale was in the genital area—either inside the "secret" crotch pocket found in most brand-name briefs or stuffed into the anal cavity. Both spots make police discovery difficult—especially in colder winter months when multiple layers of clothing serve as a buffer. Moreover, strip searches technically are barred in the St. Louis jurisdiction unless police have direct observational evidence of a dealer placing drugs in "private places." Even then, the suspect has to be arrested, booked, and then searched at the station. This is a time-consuming process, and officers will very often forgo it.

A number of offenders were aware that public strip searches were officially prohibited. "They can't make you do that [a public strip search]," explained K-Rock in lawyerlike cadence. "You can beat the case 'cause they broke the law theyself—make you pull your pants down in front of every-body. There be all kinds of witnesses. They [circuit attorneys] gonna throw out the case." This does not mean that the police do not carry out public strip searches. I myself was strip-searched during a traffic stop with an informant. Some officers have perfected a technique that avoids the need for the strip search: they slide the edge of their open hand forcibly upward from outside the offender's clothing into his crotch and rectal areas. Its noninvasiveness and perceived utility in detecting caches of rocks of varying sizes make it popular among officers who "know" a particular suspect was dealing but for situational or legal reasons cannot make the suspect disrobe on site. One offender claimed officers who used such a technique busted him with an eight-ball (about three grams) right after he had reupped, a seemingly exaggerated quantity of drugs but not out of the realm of possibility at certain times of the month.

TRANSACTIONAL MEDIATION

Dealers face the most risk of detection in the moments before and during a sale. Although police seldom arrive at the exact moment sales are made, the mere fear of that event occurring leads sellers to develop rudimentary schemes to mislead police and make it difficult for them to document a buy.[6] The *transactional mediation* schemes designed by sellers in this study were geared to minimize copresence with buyers and obfuscate hand-to-hand exchanges of money for drugs. Such schemes are "elastic yet standardized" and create role structures that make them workable in a variety of situations.[7] Performances often enlist active participation from drug customers, illustrating Goffman's seminal notion that those who share discreditability can rely on mutual aid in "passing" as normals.[8] Since crack buyers tend to be repeat customers, the schemes were commonly understood as "recipes for social action"[9] with generalized subcultural currency. Mediation using props, for example, went something like the following:

I'll tell the guy [buyer] to give me the money and go "stand on the post." The post is the *Post Dispatch* newspaper, and I'll put his rocks inside it layin' on the street a ways down the block. He knows what I means when I tell him that and trusts me 'cause I never burned him. After I do it, he goes and gets his rocks, I get my money and burn out [leave and nobody knows there was just a deal that went down]. (Blockett)

Other schemes followed the same general pattern but used different props. Dealers placed rocks in 40-ounce malt liquor caps somewhere on the ground, under bottles, or in paper bags leaning against curbs at prespecified angles, on certain newspaper stands, or simply on the ground. Buyers were told exactly what to look for: "The stones are set up in a very particular way, and only the dope fiend knows exactly what to look for because I put 'em like that and tell him," explained Blockett. Alternatively, a seller might drop the rock somewhere on the ground as he approached a user (but before establishing copresence), take the money in a furtive hand-off, and go on his way. Obviously, these and other mediational ploys described herein can be used only when competition is low and when sellers have cultivated some degree of brand loyalty with users. As demand continues to decline, this confluence will likely become increasingly uncommon, particularly in the near term.

The "flash decoy" was a mediational tactic associated with vehicle sales. Taxicabs would be used in a delivery service capacity, or dealers would be picked up by buyers and driven around to complete transactions. Unlike mediation using props, this tactic could be exercised irrespective of brand loyalty or competition: rushing headlong to a car sale, for example, one seller could reach the customer first, gain entry, and wedge off others. If pulled over by police during the drive, both parties have built-in excuses, such as, "We were ridin' to the market" (Smackhead) or "he was givin' me a lift down the set to my partner" (Knocked Out). Any dope on either party's person could be swallowed, jammed up one's anus, or stuffed into secret "stash spots" within the vehicle. Nonetheless, doing the sale in this manner can be dicey for both buyer and seller—given the mutual fear of being robbed and the compressed time frame in which vital decisions have to be made. And even if sellers manage to avoid being caught with contraband, being pulled over could be enough to get them arrested if, for example, they had an outstanding warrant, which many did.[10]

Sleight of hand is another reported mediational tactic. Though not mediation in the strict sense, it offers the illusion of such. In the world of apprehension avoidance, illusions can be as good as the real thing. The simplest forms involved "high-fives," hand slaps, and hugs—each obscuring hand-to-hand exchanges through apparent displays of affection. As one respondent illustrated:

Yeah, man, you just make it look like you be sayin', "Wussup?" with a friend. You know—slappin' hands, doin' high fives, hand-shakes, hugs, and shit. Like you and he be kin or somethin'. But what you be really doin' is exchangin' rocks and money.

Such tactics also can integrate props or recreational activity for obfuscational purposes:

I used to sell rocks out of Boston Baked Bean candy boxes [small boxes containing chocolate-covered peanuts]. The boxes would open on each end, so I'd put some rocks in one end [presumably with some covering plastic wrap in between the candy and the crack], and the candy'd be at the other. I'd act like I be eatin' the candy [as he talked, he motioned putting the box to his mouth and emptying part of its contents as if he were drinking from a soda can], but when them cluckers came along, I'd just open the other end and sell rocks out of that box. All the while, it'd just be lookin' like I be eatin' those candies [out of a box that has a "Say no to drugs!" message imprinted with boldface capital letters on the inside lid]. (Kenny)

I be playin' basketball and makin' sales while I playin'. Dope fiend walks by, and I be shootin' or somethin'. "You up?" he say. That mean do I got some [crack to sell]? He come over. I shake his hand and pass the rocks as he slides the money in my hoodie [the front pocket of his hooded sweatshirt]. (Jimmy Hat)

Perhaps the best form of mediation was ecological, involving the use of "cuts." Cuts were publicly accessible places that had a private dimension by being "off the beaten path." Cuts were largely unidentifiable to the uninitiated and not overly available to the undesired[11]—creating an ideal context in which to make a hand-to-hand exchange. Cuts included locations such as gangways, basement pits, vacant lots, alleyways, and spaces behind or between buildings. In black clothing, under cover of darkness, late at night, a seller could make himself all but invisible. Customers might learn of his presence there only after being summoned. Copresence could be established and terminated, as each party faded quickly back into obscurity. "I get on my black-hooded sweatshirt—an all-black outfit [pants and shoes]," illustrated Pee Wee Dancer. "I be in a cut, once I see poh-lice, I get back a little so they still won't peep me."

Cuts were doubly useful in their purported capacity to filter out undercover police who were posing as users. Dealers perceive undercover narcs as always wanting to be in control of a transaction—dictating where, when, and under what circumstances it will occur. Narcs also were perceived to have back-up teams with whom they needed to be in constant visual contact; strategies used to interfere with this mandate allegedly were effective in inducing suspicious behavior. Telling buyers to "come inside," "around back," or "over here" (for example, behind trees) created the kind of filter dealers needed to confirm or gainsay their suspicions. Dealers also knew that undercover officers often use marked money for transactions. Such money either has serial numbers recorded before transactions or is doused with an invisible dye that rubs off on persons who handle it. (The dye can subsequently be seen with a special light.) Using a particular cut allows dealers the extra moment to run and exchange the marked money at a local market, wash the dye from their hands, or give the cash to a fellow dealer who is not under scrutiny. As one respondent explained:

You just give it [marked money] to one of your partners real quick and without them [police] seein' you do it. They got a description of you, swerve on you, and sweat you and shit, but they ain't got nothin' 'cause my partner walked away with it [money]. That dye might show up, but you ain't got the money, so they don't got no evidence.

Seemingly lost on a number of offenders, however, was the conventional wisdom among many uniformed drug control officers; it holds that the only persons likely to be using such cuts are those with something to hide. Very much like sociologists who study deviant behavior because people often reveal themselves best in their "back alleys,"[12] police take the same approach, literally and figuratively, to nab would-be offenders. Officers patient enough to document the location of an active cut can creep up and ensnare unsuspecting offenders, providing little chance of escape. "Alleys are the place I get most of my good busts," remarked one officer.

A number of offenders corroborated the effectiveness of this police strategy, even as they lauded the insulation cuts allegedly provided. Selling from behind a building, Pee Wee

Dancer was surprised by police who suddenly appeared with guns drawn, yelling, "Freeze!" "There was nothing we could do," he said despondently. On another occasion, one of his associates was caught off guard as he walked through an alley immediately after reupping. With no time to run—much less dispose of the ten $20 rocks he was holding in his hand—he reportedly "just dropped it [the stash] on the ground. Didn't try to run or nothin'. They had me." Finally, Double-D Loc explained how he was "fixing to serve a customer out the back of a house in an alley when one time [police] roll by and peeped me [about to make the sale]. He [the officer] backed up, and I had to run. . . . He chase me in his car." Double-D Loc, however, was able to get away, throw his cache of contraband into some bushes during the chase, and retrieve it when the coast was clear.

Those with as much to hide as these offenders may have been better served by demarginalizing their behavior—taking transactions off the streets and integrating them into legitimate contexts where drug sales do not stand out as much. A number of *organizational foci*—or entities around which joint activities revolve—are "diffuse" in the sense that interactions within and around them are fleeting and not subject to intense supervision.[13] Participants eat or shop and leave, generally being indifferent to the activities of unknown others. Such places also are self-contained and ostensibly private, providing a contextual buffer and greater protection from police intrusion. Vulnerability decreases proportionately with recourse to such places.

Lacking the most basic social capital and dramaturgical skills, however, only a handful of dealers claimed to use these legitimate contexts on a frequent or successful basis. K-Rock, an older, more experienced, and more "successful" seller within the set, was one of them. He recounts an occasion where he worked off his pager to meet a customer at a local fast-food restaurant:

I just go up to Wendy's, and he [the customer] be up there. He act like he orderin' somethin', and I just sit down at one of the tables, and then he sit down with his food. He tells you already that the money be on the table, and you just slip him the shit during the conversation, like all natural and stuff, like you just be hangin' out. Play like you fixin' to eat and like you supposed to be together. Leave with him and then [go] where you gotta go.

Similarly, Benzo explained how he would sell crack out of a candy store near his parents' home—either waiting inside for customers to signal him or loitering out front to catch buyers as they passed by:

Most of the time, I be at the store, the candy store, goin' in and out buyin' stuff [candy, chips, soda, etc.] so nobody trip out. If I be inside, dope fiend look through the glass and see me and gimme a "er-eh-er!" Then I come outside and make the sale in the gangway or somethin'. Or the fiend come inside the store, and we do the transaction in there. Family friend own the store so he don't care.

TAKING FLIGHT

No matter how effectively sellers stashed their drugs, how conscientious they were about obscuring hand-to-hand exchanges, or how normal they made themselves appear, arrest avoidance came down to whether sellers could escape the clutches of police or dispose of evidence prior to being detained.

Decisions about whether and how soon to run (after coming under police scrutiny) were largely a function of how "dirty" individual sellers perceived themselves to be. This assessment was itself subjective—hinging on the amount of contraband a seller had on his person, how quickly he thought he could dispose of it, his legal status (whether he had outstanding warrants), and most important, the accessibility of escape routes. All else being equal, the more "loading" on these factors a given offender had, the more likely he was to scamper.

Composure under fire is critical, no matter how intense the scrutiny. Equanimity can preempt police suspicion, while its absence can do the opposite. To look suspicious is bad in itself, but to try to cover it up is worse. Both responses render the performance artificial and deserving of further investigation.[14] The differential enforcement practices of urban police, in which young black males are singled out as those most deserving of their attention, make the management of normal appearances only more exacting. Performance flaws are easily identifiable when the audience purposefully looks for them.[15] Jimmy Hat thus insisted that when "you see po pos [police] come on the scene, you can't nut up. You know, be nervous, lookin' at 'em out the corner your eye. You gotta be true to yours and can't let no poh-lice scare you." A-Train added, "If you jump [when police roll by, you] make 'em come to you when they ain't even thinkin' about you. You speak 'em up, 'Oh man, I'm gonna get flagged,' and get all paranoid. That's when you get [flagged]."

The offenders' reported goal, thus, was to sustain a natural and spontaneous involvement in business at hand, deflecting attention through displays of normalcy.[16] This could be arduous, however, given the confounding behavior of the crackheads they often dealt with and from whom they could not always quickly detach:

They be all fuckin' shakin'—nose runnin' and shit. You don't know what the fuck wrong with them. They crazy, like they got a disease. That shit tacky as a motherfucker. (Fade)

Emaciated, unkempt, and excitable, such purchasers draw attention as a matter of course, especially when in the company of suspected dealers. Mere copresence often provides enough police justification for a stop and search:

When poh-lice go by, they [users] nut up. They get shaky and nervous, and that make me shaky and make police think, "Hey, they lookin' suspicious. I think there's somethin' goin' on here." Then they hop out and get on us. (Ice-D)

The negative effects of such attention can be neutralized by multiple sellers united in space and time. A seller who is not "dirty," for example, might draw attention to himself to provide a decoy for others to escape:

If you ain't slingin' and your partner is, you do somethin' to make them [police] jump out and check you [and not the other guy or guys]. Start talkin' to his ass, walk in front of his car, ask 'em for a motherfuckin' baseball card. Get 'em to talk to you for awhile, blase, blase—"Just wanted a baseball card, [whatever]." Let your partner go about his business. Just walk away, real calm and slow. Ain't gotta bring no attention. Whoever don't got nothin' [isn't holding contraband] play that role. (Fade)

Multiple sellers also can act as collective decoys by taking off in separate directions all at once:

If somebody dirty and the poh-lice swoop, everybody runs. Poh-lice won't know who to go after. (Skates)

We all run, they might not get the . . . person [who is in possession]. That person gonna go stash his crack, and by the time they find out that person, he already done stash and came back. . . . We all gonna run because then poh-lice would know who had it if only one guy ran. (Tony Mack)

Dealers were somewhat "safe" in fleeing the scene, given the extreme community reactions that would result if police were to shoot to stop them.[17] Even if individual sellers were caught, the amount of crack confiscated would likely be insignificant. Whatever the case, offenders' territorial boundedness afforded significant advantage in the event they had to take flight. Endless hours on the streetcorner made sellers intimately familiar with their surroundings. Tony Mack claimed it was "easy" to get away: "Got all the cuts down 'cause it my hood. Ain't gonna catch me." Other offenders exulted similarly; a number reveled particularly at the prospect of taking flight in inclement weather:

Winter the best time. Snow, rain, and sleet, poh-lice get on you, you on your feet, you go up a street, hit a gangway, alley, they gonna tear they car up. They slide up, they skatin'. I already where I wanna be by the time they chase me for real [on foot]. (K-Rock)

Winter the best time—ain't no police feel like jumpin' out that motherfucker. Be colder than a motherfucker. Hit a couple gang-

ways, and they ass ain't gonna catch me. Can't punch no car in
gangway in the snow for real. Don't want to tear the motherfucker
up. They can run, but you faster. (Fade)

Such reports were not without merit. St. Louis City Police
officers drive late-model Chevrolet Caprices and Ford Crown
Victorias, vehicles with 305-cubic-inch front-mounted en-
gines and rear-wheel drive. From ride-alongs, I can attest per-
sonally to their complete lack of traction in wet weather, especially snow. Hitting a turn with any speed or acceleration
results in a fishtail or futile tire-spinning.

The evidence of cooperative forms of apprehension avoidance among dealers was striking, considering the every-man-
for-himself attitude that typically defined their collective selling relations. Though such cooperation was neither complex
nor well planned, it underlines the truism that internal cohesion increases in the face of external threat. Cooperation
also is consistent with previous research on youthful street
offenders—particularly gang-affiliated ones—that holds that
the sources of loyalty are exogenous rather than intrinsic. Remove the threat, and the cohesion evaporates.[18]

Whether having others around or dealing by oneself is
more likely to attract the attention that leads to the need to
scamper—excepting the obvious attention multiple sellers
rushing to customers at one place and time draws—is an in-
teresting empirical issue, but one that I cannot answer defini-
tively. As one dealer arguing for lone dealing explained,
"Who you think they [police] gonna fuck with more—a
whole group of niggas or one just sittin' by hisself? Who
draws more attention?" As Skates put it, "When you walkin'
in a group, poh-lice really sweat you. When you walkin' by
yoself, they don't really trip off you." Double-D Loc observed,
"I mostly be by myself or with another person. It's better
to be with two people. Four or more draw attention, draws
police, where with two, it look like you just be walking down
the street, like you be friends, just chillin'." Other dealers
countered that larger groups of individuals—regardless of
whether all were selling—afforded more protection because

one could "slink off in the distance" while the police were dealing with the crowd. Large groups can dilute the focus on any one person and create a diversionary window of opportunity for escape.

DISPOSING OF EVIDENCE

To be apprehended is one thing; to be apprehended with drug evidence is far more serious. Given that oral stashing is the preferred mode of hiding the on-person inventory, and given that sellers could not or did not run with the approach of every police car, the strategic decision came down to when to swallow the evidence. There were five possibilities: swallow the rocks (1) as soon as police cars were seen to enter and stop in the immediate dealing vicinity, (2) after officers stepped from their patrol cars and approached on foot, (3) after officers exited their cars in ways that made it appear as if a search was imminent (such as getting out fast, rushing up to offenders, telling them to freeze), (4) after approaching officers were recognized as being especially tough-minded, or (5) after police entered offenders' personal space and ordered their mouths opened. Generally speaking, the risk of arrest increases with each stage of delay.

Delays can be disastrous—particularly if a dealer overestimates his own acuity or underestimates that of police. Ice-D, for example, described being caught off guard after electing to "feel out" the officer in question instead of swallowing his cache immediately:

I had it in my mouth, and poh-lice grabbed me so quick [by the neck in a frontal choke hold] I couldn't swallow it [the stash]! Stuck his finger in my mouth, and he got it.

Preemptive swallowing is perhaps the least desirable but safest option—least desirable because the stash has to be ingested, safest because police have no evidence to seize. Assuming that the cellophane housing prevents rocks from breaking down and leeching into offenders' digestive tracts, sellers can vomit them up later. This compromises neither their fiscal position nor their physical well-being. A variety of techniques and home remedies reportedly are effective in inducing vomit. Some dealers stress the importance of always eating or drinking something before going out to sell. The idea is to have something of mass in one's stomach—a medium—that can surround the rocks and subsequently be expelled intact:

If you don't eat nothin', it hard to get them birds back up. You ain't got nothin' in your stomach to throw up. If you have to swallow, go in and eat, wait thirty minutes, go in the bathroom, and throw it up. Might not get all of 'em back but the majority [will come back]. (Skates)

Always eat somethin' before I go outside [to sell]. You gotta empty stomach, you throw up all water. It don't come up right. Food, it wrap 'round the dope. You throws up, and the food pushes it up [and out]. (Deuce Low)

Double-D Loc, by contrast, described a homemade emetic he whipped up and drank at the first available opportunity after swallowing—a concoction he claimed would rapidly induce a successful discharge:

You just drink some vinegar with some baking soda, maybe a teaspoon of soda. It boils up down there and erupts your stomach, make you cough it up.

K-Rock claimed such measures were unnecessary and that how one swallowed was more important than some crudely fashioned recipe to induce vomiting. As he saw it, controlling one's swallow—not letting rocks go "all the way down" but having them lodge somewhere in the esophageal corridor— was the way to do this:

You know how when you swallow an aspirin [a $20 rock is nearly the same size] and it get stuck in your throat, it don't go all the way down? That's how I swallow my rocks. I swallow one at a time. Just like a motherfuckin' aspirin, as soon as I get flagged [stopped by police]. [When police leave], I just stick my finger down there, and they come right back up.

The offenders spoke of such issues with the matter-of-factness of a family doctor, acknowledging none of the physical discomfort or disgust associated with a forced retching. Whatever else one wants to say, these are the effects of drug control policy as they are played out on the streets.

CONCLUSION

Engaged principally in an instrumental, economic activity, curbside drug sellers develop and implement strategies that are least disruptive to business yet provide the maximum amount of insulation from arrest.[19] The practices discussed in this chapter are a direct, situational response to police initiatives intended to "dramatically increase [offenders'] perceived and/or actual threat of apprehension."[20] Of course, social control policies and offenders' responses to them are dynamic. Conflicting parties change strategy over time to meet emergent challenges. As Ryan observes, the "interaction of law enforcers and deviants produces a dialectical process of change, each side responding to the moves of the other by altering its social organization and personnel."[21] Police make inroads, crack dealers adapt and change, and police change again, as the competition to outsmart one another continuously cycles.

Some researchers suggest that the widely reported attitude of indifference about arrest among active street-offender populations is a function of their perceived ability to outsmart the police.[22] This assessment is not without merit—particularly for drug dealers. The average heroin seller, for example, is arrested only once every twelve months. Many are never arrested during the course of a year's selling.[23] For curbside crack sellers, only one arrest occurs for every 200 transactions.[24] Among drug-market participants in general, rates of arrest range from one in every 353 crimes to one in every 413—unimpressive at best.[25] This is not to say that such figures are broadly representative or predictive, or that offenders lack a fear of arrest. The evasionary strategies outlined in this chapter underscore the role of threat in energizing behavior to avoid apprehension.

One could make the alternative argument that attitudes of indifference are an effect rather than the cause of offenders' arrest-avoidance strategies: some offenders may believe themselves to be so immune from detection because of their self-proclaimed elusiveness that nothing deters them from selling—even the most intense police initiatives. The fact that legal sanctions are not especially intimidating reinforces this perceptual stance: for most street cases, incarceration is likely to be brief, and periodic bouts of jail time often can provide a welcome respite from the dog-eat-dog world of the streetcorner.[26] This is not to say that offenders will not take any and all necessary measures to avoid arrest, but rather to suggest that most realistically recognize that it is only a matter of time before they fall prey to the "bitch of chance."[27]

It is traditionally thought that vertical business models of distribution facilitate arrest avoidance best since a variety of roles can be performed by multiple and dispersed individuals. Drugs and money are separated so the aggregate amount of seizable contraband becomes diffused. But the lack of social organization and poor management skills of most curbside freelance sellers may lead them to unwittingly enjoy the same benefits of diffusion. Small enclaves of sellers dispersed throughout a drug set require expensive and time-consuming "duplicate observational processes" by police. This makes systematic surveillance and apprehension difficult.[28] Multiple sellers converging in space and time present the same dilemma, given the relative ease with which sellers can scatter, use decoys, and dispose of evidence. Chasing individual sellers may not be worth the effort, since the amounts likely to be confiscated are meager. In the end, crackdowns, sweeps, and the like will be plagued by their inability to catch more than a few individuals at a time—each with insignificant amounts of contraband.[29]

As curbside crack markets continue to stagnate and decline, the effectiveness of the arrest-avoidance strategies outlined in this chapter arguably may wane as well. Stifling competition, indiscreet selling, low demand, and a fixed police presence increase risk no matter how skilled a seller thinks he is in avoiding detection. In the near term, aggressive sellers are likely to do well financially (by rushing customers and stealing sales), but they also will be most prone to being weeded out first. Discreet sellers who fill their shoes can capitalize on the indirect "experiential effects"[30] and refine their tactics accordingly. Basic principles of evolutionary adaptation and succession in declining, resource-scarce environments, however, suggest that once passive sellers may become highly aggressive when highly aggressive others have been removed, holding the level of competition constant. The opportunity cost of not "seizing the moment"—no matter how high the risk—may be too substantial to forgo. The cycle of succession and adaptation will continue unless and until an upper limit for competition intersects with a lower one for demand. At this point, the practicality of selling crack on the streetcorner evaporates. Whether would-be sellers find alternative sources of illicit income or are absorbed into the legal economy are separate issues, to be pursued in the concluding chapter.

6 Undercover Police

Given the tactics that street crack sellers use to avoid arrest, urban police must anticipate their schemes and find effective strategies to apprehend them. Undercover operations provide just such a method. As proactive law enforcers seeking to prevent expected crimes from occurring, undercover officers are immersed in fictitious identities to infiltrate settings otherwise inaccessible to formal social control. Central to the success of any operative is the ability to deceive those targeted for investigation. Accomplishing this requires officers to perform their criminal personas as credibly as possible: credibility is the necessary and sufficient condition for infiltration.

This performance task in itself is onerous, and barriers to entry into the illicit drug subculture make it even more so. Research across time and place indicates that drug sellers are "reluctant to sell to anyone who is not an established and recognized customer or, in their perception, someone who is not an obvious addict."[1] Yet this reluctance tends to lessen as one moves down the dealing chain, where financial need becomes pressing. The urgency to increase revenue is particularly strong on the streetcorner and in a declining market. Here, sellers may be more willing to take a chance on the unfamiliar.

Chance-taking is by no means an irrational process. Curbside drug dealers are renowned for their alleged ability to read

and interpret "vibes" that tell them whether a potential customer is "OK."[2] Indeed, the prevailing sentiment among
street sellers is that they can "smell the poh-lice" a mile away.
This is generally a function of deception clues only undercover officers are perceived to leak. By screening for such
clues, offenders can preempt sales that might otherwise lead
to arrest.[3] This chapter explores the form and content of these
clues.

SCANNING

Though influxes of unfamiliar customers in declining markets are not common, "new" users can and do appear. They
may be people who generally purchase elsewhere, referrals
from existing customers, or the infrequent neophytes looking
to score. To purchase crack successfully, potential buyers
must comprehend and then enact a rather detailed set of conduct norms that guide both verbal and nonverbal behavior.
Like most expectations of conduct, such norms become visible
only when someone fails to enact them correctly. Violators of
these conduct norms do not have a good chance of coming
away with the desired product.

   No transaction is initiated before buyers and sellers first
scan the environment—and each other.[4] *Scanning*—obtaining an overview of a person's projected appearance and general demeanor—is critical for establishing a mutual interest
in doing business. The customers' way of driving, walking,
and gazing all portend a potential sale if done in proper fashion. If done improperly, transactions might be preempted
even though both parties actually want to complete a sale. In
normal life, looking too long at someone in any public environment violates etiquette and requires corrective behavior.
In the street-level crack scene, however, staring has fundamental implications for whether transactions have any chance
for initiation and completion. "Mutually understood signals
must be conveyed, intentions expressed, and [actions] sus-

tained by reciprocal encouragement."[5] The mutual glance—distinct from simple sightings or observations—serves this purpose and "signifies a wholly new and unique union" between prospective, illicit transaction partners.[6]

Dealers know that people in cars who drive relatively fast, avert their eyes, or gaze only in civil inattention are not interested in buying crack. Vehicular buyers have come for a reason and will slow down to "scope out" persons milling about the streets for signs of reciprocal interest. Drivers may ride around for a short period of time to try to spot law enforcement personnel and then return, stare, stop, and wait for someone to approach them. Alternatively, they may drive up to a group of suspected dealers and initiate interaction themselves. Buyers on foot use the same general approach but usually are more direct in approaching the vicinity of suspected dealers—prequalifying the area for the absence of law enforcement through a simple head check. Again, mutual gazing plays a critical role in determining whether transactions are initiated.

At this point, dealers' "perceptual shorthand"[7] comes into play, telling them, first, whether to approach and, second, how to organize the interaction in ways that maximize their chances of avoiding a sale that could lead to arrest. Whether to approach potential customers is a function of physical clues. Whether to proceed with transactions is a function of verbal clues and their corroboration or contradiction of physical ones.

PHYSICAL CLUES

Unlike other drugs, crack is unique by virtue of its debilitating effect on users. The binging behavior associated with many street-level crack consumers—whom these sellers modally served—tends to cause progressive wasting and physical emaciation.[8] "Cluckers," as sellers refer to such persons, are reportedly easy to identify even if specific information about the person's identity is unknown. "They be all toe down and raggedy, 'specially the girls," remarked C-Dogg. "Their booty [buttocks] sink in, and they lose their titties— look stupid, you know." Added Snap-boy, "They be all snifflin' and their nose runnin' and shit. Look like they got their clothes out the trash." "You can tell a fiend from a mile away," another seller insisted. "Someone who looks like they lost a lot of weight, got on some raggedy clothes. They really don't care about theyself. They dirty all the time."[9] Such tell-tale signs are particularly evident among users "geeking" for another hit. "They eyes be all glazed and big and shit," Blockett remarked. "You know how them—what do you call 'em?—pupils get all big. That's what they look like when they be geekin' for more of that crack."

Features seen up close that were significant markers of ongoing crack use were black, sootlike stains and calloused crud on hands and fingers from repetitive lighting of straight shooters (small metallic, glass, or porcelain straws used to smoke crack; they are sometimes called *stems*). Burns, blisters, and lip sores also might be apparent from compulsive smoking: when crack users run out of either money or crack, they can continue to get high by scraping resin off the side of the stem, pushing the screen through to the other side where more resin has accumulated, repacking the screen with the scraped-off resin, and lighting it again. This can make the pipe tremendously hot. Some users also reportedly have pock-marks and open cuts on their faces and arms, bite impressions on their lips, and scratches on their necks as a result of compulsive "tweeking" (picking behavior during or after use).

Dealers claimed it is too difficult for an undercover police officer to imitate these characteristics. "Poh-lice try to copy it, but the behavior be fake. They be tryin' too hard, shakin' too hard, tryin' to stutter, bendin' all over and shit, but their eyes be too clear to really be geekin'," explained one respondent. But not all cluckers or, for that matter, all crack users fit the above profile. For those who are not emaciated, geeking, or glazed, other appearance-based clues are "peeped," as dealers put it, to gauge credibility. One such clue was "big-ass shirts or jackets" that can conceal either microphone wires or bulletproof vests. (In the very first stages of this research, I was told to lift up my shirt to demonstrate that I was not wired.) Another clue was buyers who tried to dress like dope fiends but somehow did not fit the part. "All you gotta do is picture 'em in decent clothes, and you can tell somethin' ain't right," said one respondent. A final clue involved the cadence and stride of a prospective buyer's walk. A policeman's walk, remarked one respondent,

ain't like everyone else's walk. It's a certain kind of perfect walk, a cocky walk, like they know they gonna arrest your ass and take you to jail.

One of Johnson and Natarajan's respondents explained the "giveaway factor" more succinctly:

You can just tell. It's the way they carry themselves. It's the way they act, the way they look, the way they dress—everything. They just don't, they just don't know how to work the street. They don't know how to be, you know, "down." . . . When you on the street long enough, you learn to pick up the scent.[10]

For dealers who sell to customers in cars, attention is paid to everything about the vehicle—both outside and in. Four-door vehicles and vans are regarded as particularly suspicious because they can hide several crouching police officers. Vehicles with tinted windows and antennae (either telephone or citizens band) also are carefully scrutinized. Cars and vans with no front plates or rear registration stickers are widely regarded as SCAT cars, making their use little different from that of regular black-and-whites.[11] Fancy late-model cars are seen as more suspicious than clunkers. As one dealer put it, "Where's a clucker gonna get the money to buy some nice car if he spendin' all his money on rock?" Indeed, a crack addiction can put one in dire financial straits. One respondent claimed that one of his customers had traded her children's Christmas presents for rocks. Another clucker was purported to have accepted $20 from a dealer to beat up the mother of that dealer. Humiliating, crack-induced sexual missions for money also are commonly reported.

If vehicles pass initial muster, close attention then is paid to their interior. As Smackman explained:

The first thing you look at is the dash. See if there's a CB or phone. Then you be peepin' the floor and all around under the seats for straps [guns] or any kind of wires. You be watchin' the guy all the time, seein' if he got any plug [for a wire] in his ear, seein' how he's actin', seein' if he be reachin' for anything suspicious or if he be actin' all janky [suspicious].

A certain raggedness to the car's inside also was expected. Cigarette butts and trash strewn about the vehicle and the noxious smell of alcohol mixed with perspiration all were signs leading toward an assessment of transactional safety.

Some may argue that the physical clues apply only to the gross distinction between hard-core dope fiends and undercover cops trying to mimic them and that, in reality, customers in many drug-selling locales are not "fiends" but "normal-looking" people who want to get high. Nevertheless, buyers who do not display outward signs of decrepitude are "risky" because they deviate from typifications of what street-level crack users "should" look like. This is especially true in a stagnating, central-city, curbside market—where demand has matured and street users often are in advanced stages of addiction. Whether sellers take a chance on such persons is a decision ultimately determined by verbal clues.

DIALOGIC INITIATION: VERBAL CLUES

The point at which seller and buyer engage each other verbally is the most critical juncture in the strategic interaction. It is at this point that dealers report being able to discern the difference between real buyers and pretenders. No matter how credible their physical portrayal, there reportedly were subtleties in what legitimate buyers said and how they said it—as opposed to "intruders" unfamiliar with the subculture who tried to affect the argot—that tipped off dealers that something "just wasn't right."

Verbal illegitimacy centered on two things—substance and style. Soliciting crack "improperly" involved (1) unacceptable ways of asking for transactions, which included incorrect references to the drug itself, and (2) unacceptable stylistic ways of conducting transactions.

Unacceptable ways of asking for transactions were easily identifiable and reported in the following forms:

"Do you know where I can get some drugs around here?"
"Who's got the dope around here?"
"Can I get somethin' for a twenty?"
"Lemme see somethin' for fifty."
"You know where I can get crack from around here?"
"Anybody gotta rock?"
"Can I get a bopper for fifty dollars?"

Such inquiries showed a lack of understanding of proper solicitational argot—a shortcoming associated with undercover police. A bopper, for example, refers to ten $20 rocks and would cost $200 not $50. "Do you know where I can get some drugs around here?" is suspicious because, as one respondent put it, "Why would he come on the set if he didn't know there was dope there in the first place?" The "Can I get somethin' for a twenty?" and "Lemme see somethin' for fifty" lines were perceived as entrapment devices in which officers attempted to induce voluntary references to the fact that dealers did indeed have crack on their person and were willing to sell it. References to crack as "crack" or "rock" in most forms of inquiry were inappropriate and raised suspicion because it was just not the way things were done.

Credible modes of actual solicitation, in contrast, were less obtrusive, more indirect, and seemingly vague to someone not privy to subcultural knowledge: the more meandering the inquiry, the less threatened dealers felt and the more inclined they would be to proceed with a transaction. Coded dialogue was reportedly effective in this regard. Veiled substantive references to crack (such as "stones," "rack," "ya," or "girl"), numerical quantities of crack spelled out (two-oh for a $20 stone; four-oh for $40), or camouflaged inquiries infused with transactional subtext all were appropriate. Jimmy Hat expounds on the latter:

Dope fiend might come up and say he gonna bet me twenty dollars he can beat me [in a game of basketball]. That means he want a twenty-dollar stone. Or "Lemme shoot the ball against you for a hundred dollars." That mean he want somethin' for a hundred. [If] he say, "I wanna five" [$5 rock], I say, "I don't know what you talkin' about."

The following modes of solicitation typically were considered the most acceptable:

"Is you on the clock?"
"Is you handlin'?"
"Is you cool?"
"Is you workin'?"
"You up?"
"Got some work?"
"Come holler at me."
"Can I holler at ya?"
"Wussup?"
"Wussup cuz?"

Such forms of talk "provide a means for negotiating encounters with strangers" and "become tools for gauging intent." [12] More important, these were inquiries that dealers believed only real users familiar with the nuances of subcultural jargon would know. The "Wussup?" inquiry was probably the most effective one in prequalifying potential buyers and determining through their response whether they were legitimate. It had reciprocal dimensions to it as well: as often is the case among strangers, dealers might first say "Wussup?" to induce a confirmatory response in someone they thought to be a user looking to buy some crack. As Goffman notes, "Once this show of interest has been given, other moves can be made in order that the two might bring each other into discrete [sic] conversation. Indeed, it is structurally possible for

a [deal] to occur in a public street without third persons knowing that [one] has occurred and, furthermore, without either
end too much jeopardizing his (or her) own capacity to with-
draw at any juncture."[13]

Conversational style was the second important verbal dimension dealers looked for in making credibility assessments.
Improper style was a verbal deception clue I noted earlier,[14]
but that report pertained to "transactional pushiness"—the
idea of being overanxious to purchase drugs during a negotiation. Though transactional pushiness was not central here, a
number of other linguistic miscues were reported. As Sisco
described:

Even if they have the street lingo down, there's somethin' about the
way they talk that makes you think they've been *trained* to talk
that way, like it's not part of their everyday thing. They may got
the words but not the feelin' in the words.

Luther reported that police would attempt to appear part of
the drug scene by making up stories they thought would facilitate infiltration. One such tactic was for officers to say they
just got "ganked" (burned, robbed) down the street and
needed to hook up this time with real dope. The way they
voiced this allegation, however, was not credible:

The poh-lice be all calm and shit when they say they just got
ganked by somebody else and wanted another stone. A real dope
fiend wouldn't come back for another twenty because he could get
ganked again right off [and probably wouldn't have the money
anyway]. And if he did come back, he'd be all pissed off and shit,
talkin' all fast, stutterin', not all calm like the poh-lice be.

Luther also reported that suspected officers would attempt
to lengthen conversations—something not natural to street
crack transactions, which demand brevity, furtiveness, and
terse speech:

They [perceived police] talk a lot when they tryin' to buy. They try
to get you to have a whole conversation goin'. They just wanna talk
and talk and talk, but what they really be doin' is pumpin' you for

information, seein' who you hang with and where, and to get you
to talk about dealin' so they get you on tape [through a wire].

Smackman agreed:

They be trippin' more on you than the dope, you know, talkin' to
ya, "Blah, blah, blah." Real dope fiends never do that. They just
wanna get their stones and go 'cause they wanna get high and they
be just as worried about the poh-lice as we be.

A final verbal red flag involved something suspected undercover officers refrained from doing—specifically, the way
in which they failed to negotiate deals. A number of respondents claimed that cops, unlike users, would not try to "work"
for the best deal possible. Users were notorious for trying
to buy the most rocks for the least money and had various
schemes for doing so. As one offender describes:

Dope fiends got all the games down right. Like they come to you
for a twenty but only have fi'teen on them. So you give 'em a
twenty 'cause it's close enough. Then, ten minutes later, they come
back with eight bones [dollars] and ask if you can hook them up
with a dime [a ten-dollar rock]. They end up gettin' thirty dollars'
worth for twenty-three dollars.

Other negotiation tactics commonly used by "real" users
were asking for dope on credit and attempting to win price
reductions for volume buys (both of which suspected police
reportedly did not do). As LeShawn put it, "If I could tell
the poh-lice to do one thing that would make me think they
were cool to sell to, it would be to bring like thirty dollars'
or thirty-five dollars' worth instead of always twenties and
forties." Asking for two $20 rocks and then offering $35
or less is effective because it demonstrates desperation for
the best deal possible—a hustle commonly played out by
street-level drug users who seek the maximum high per
dollar spent. Relatedly, the *kind* of money suspected police
present also was important. "They'll give you the crispiest
motherfuckin' bills in the world," Blockett exclaimed. Real
"clucker money" is dirty, torn, crumpled, boxed, or balled to

fit in the palm of one's hand and, as a consequence, often is sweaty and soiled. Very small denominations, such as loose change, rolled-up quarters, and $1 bills toted in plastic grocery bags taken from Dumpsters also may be used to pay for rocks. Perceived narcs reportedly did not go to such lengths because they did not, financially, have to. Credible physical presentations could leak deception by ignoring attention to detail.

TESTS

If still in doubt about a buyer's legitimacy, dealers might proceed to test him or her in various ways. Perhaps the most extreme method involved forced drug use on the spot. "I'll tell him to hit the straight shooter [inhale crack smoke through a lit glass pipe], and if he do, then I know he cool." This method carries obvious risks, however. If buyers are indeed police, dealers can be arrested immediately for possession. Further, undercover officers have an assortment of methods to circumvent this situation (including simulation and excuses)—allowing transactional completion and investigational continuance.

A less extreme test used by dealers (albeit with the risk of a possession charge) was to produce a rock far smaller than that solicited to see how the buyer would react. A skeptical dealer, for example, might offer a $5 or $10 rock instead of the $20 stone requested. "If he take it and pay you for it," explained one respondent, "you think he be poh-lice. No real dope fiend gonna give you twenty dollars for a nickel [$5 rock]. They gonna get what they pay for." And if a dealer was arrested as a result of that sale, it would likely be for simple possession rather than felony distribution. As Knocked-out put it, "I be back out in twenty-fo' [24 hours]."

Whether buyers attempted to scrutinize the requested merchandise or taste rocks was also an important signal of credibility. Placed momentarily on the tongue, crack produces an immediate numbing sensation—a crude but effective indicator of its authenticity (even though other cutting agents—such as lidocaine, procaine, and novocaine—can mimic this numbing sensation without bearing psychoactive properties). But as one respondent remarked, "No cop gonna taste that dope. They think it gonna kill 'em or somethin'."

A final test dealers employed was to ask prospective buyers for the names of other people that buyers knew in the neighborhood to see whether they could name and describe specific people with whom they had dealt before. "Yeah man, if I ain't seen the guy around before, I'll ask him to describe someone they had dealt with before. They'll give you a name, sayin' somethin' like 'I know so-and-so' and then you say somethin' like, 'Does he have a fro, box, or bob [three different haircut styles]? Is he brown, dark, or light skinned?' Stuff like that. If he be givin' you the right answers, then you think he be OK." Of course, such a buyer could very well be a skilled undercover officer who had "knocked up" (arrested and interrogated) the person he claimed to know or a user turned informant coached by undercover officers (a strategy against which dealers admittedly had little defense). Nevertheless, suspicions could be either confirmed or allayed by such responses, a process manipulated by particularly savvy dealers who might try to trip up someone they suspect. As Blast explained:

Yeah man, if you don't know 'em but think they might be cool, you ask 'em about diff'rent people in the neighborhood, like who they know. Or you ask 'em about a particular person you make up that doesn't really exist. Like this one guy who wanted to buy, I started talkin' about this dude Terry [a person who allegedly lived down the street but was fictional] and whether he knew him. He said, "Yeah, yeah, I know him. He's cool." I started makin' all this shit up like, "I heard Terry got some fire [guns]," and was goin' on about all the different kinds he got. Then I started talkin' about his new Cadillac and how nice it was. All the while he be agreein' to everythin' I be talkin' about and none of it be true. There wasn't no Terry, he didn't have no guns or Cadillac, so I think he [the buyer] be the poh-lice.

CONCLUSION

For practical, political, and symbolic reasons, streetcorner crack sellers are the most vulnerable of illicit drug dealers to undercover infiltrations. Local narcotics police generally effect the greatest presence among street-level vendors because of their obtrusiveness and their accessibility relative to dealers at higher rungs. Large numbers of drug arrests, which low-level dealers can readily provide, have immediate value to authorities seeking to prove they are tough on drugs. Crack's destructive effects on both people and communities energize already zealous activity designed to stamp out these offenders. Likened to malicious vectors of the most virulent of pests, curbside crack sellers have become a favorite target of police and politicians alike.[15]

An ease-of-infiltration hypothesis, however, is not supported by my research findings. Sellers demonstrate the undeniable ability to identify suspected police and refuse sales to them. The perceptual skills required to do this—honed from weeks, months, and sometimes years of life on the streetcorner—allow them to distinguish the "normal" from the "pathological":[16] true dope fiends talk, act, and look a "certain way," and dealers felt they could "tell" real ones from fakes. Theoretically, their shorthand is grounded in Gibbs's notion of "restrictive deterrence," which refers to the ways in which criminals reduce their overall offense frequencies to evade detection, identification, and apprehension.[17]

Gibbs speculated that "some individuals curtail their violations of law in the belief that repetition is likely to result eventually in their suffering of punishment."[18] Probabilities, he implies, constitute the basis for restrictive deterrence. The data presented here indicate that restrictive deterrence was a tactical choice and not a fatalistic tradeoff. Conspicuously absent was the mentality that "I better not sell to this guy because I've sold to too many people already and my number could be up." Rather, strategic analysis of deception clues available within any given drug transaction was the modality of criminal restraint.[19] Both forms speak strongly to the fact that objective sanction properties alone cannot explain the operation of deterrence.[20] Indeed, the principle that fear of harsh punishment[21] acts as the primary crime prevention mechanism makes little empirical sense in light of the available techniques criminals can use prospectively to evade apprehension. The dealers I interviewed did not fear being ensnared by some undercover net. They sincerely believed they could weed out charlatans before any damage could be done.

Although restrictively deterrent measures may reduce the absolute number of criminal offenses, they also, paradoxically, may cause offenders to become further engulfed in deviant roles.[22] Insularity from outsiders means an increasing isolation from conventional society and greater cohesiveness with cooffenders and the offending lifestyle. The frequency of deviant acts may decrease, but the intensity of identification with other crack market participants may do just the opposite.[23]

In declining markets, the benefits of perceptually filtering customers may be increasingly outweighed by their cost. Unknown numbers of persons who have no law enforcement affiliation but may wish to try crack may be turned away empty-handed because they are not emaciated or poor, do not have the right skin color, or do not know the proper transactional argot. These are false positives that result in lost sales that could have been completed with little risk of incurring legal sanctions. In the aggregate, their effect could be profound[24]—particularly if *potential* customers (such as white suburbanites) hear they cannot buy crack because they don't fit the "crack user profile" and therefore do not try. The accessibility of curbside markets may make them the primary if not the sole option for such persons, assuming a lack of criminal capital. The extent to which unsuccessful but "wannabe" buyers—potential customers who want, or have wanted, access to crack markets but who are, or have been, cognitively locked out—contribute to drug market stagnation is an important empirical question that has yet to be answered.

Other effects of crack's decline on streetcorner markets are speculative and hard to know. The sellers who remain may represent those who are the best at filtering out undercover narcs: experience and skill accrue to those who persist and survive in high-risk settings by making rapid, precise, and accurate assessments of transactional credibility (understanding that the behavior of narcs changes over time). Alternatively, sellers who remain may be the worst—the truly desperate who will sell to anyone with money. Stifling competition, obtrusive selling arrangements, and a finite but dwindling pool of hard-core users may make such sellers increasingly prone "to dispense with [prudence] and proceed quickly at high risk."[25] The fact that thoughts about getting caught typically are dismissed in the actual offending moment would seem to facilitate this outcome.[26] This is to say nothing of the distorting influences that superoptimism, perceptions of invincibility, raw emotion, or inebriation can have on the offender decision-making process[27]—or of the widely held belief in the "quick risk" of crime, which holds that the threat of detection is small because it is over "in a flash" and thus not something to worry about.[28] Markets in decline may amplify these distortions—exacerbating the conditions that work against discretion.

7 Crack in Decline

Researchers initially thought that open-air, curbside sales would dominate urban crack markets as they had with heroin in the 1970s. Characterized by overt transactions "with apparent indifference to potential police action or other forms of legal interference,"[1] open-air marketing allows the greatest number of customers to be served per unit of time. Open-air selling also hinders police surveillance because activity is not limited to one dedicated location. Analysts also predicted that as demand matured and competition became more virulent, vertically organized business operations would direct the activities of participating sellers in the most efficient way possible. Vertical business operations are characterized by vertical differentiation, pooled interdependence, a formal multitiered system of organization, and well-defined employer-employee relationships. They enmesh sellers in complementary rather than conflictual pursuits. As functional coexistence becomes the order of the day, the odds of survival, financial and otherwise, greatly increase.[2]

Neither modality has been realized. As an organizational system, open-air selling has become a "distant third" to sellers working in crack houses and sellers working with beepers who meet customers at preassigned locations.[3] At least part of the reason for this lies in the inferior quality of the product open-air sellers are perceived to offer. Open-air sales also are risky: both purchasers and sellers can be victimized by robbers or other drug market participants at any time. Typically, one is reduced to buying street crack as the craving and need for it escalate "because using other sources require[s] some measure of gratification delay and discipline." Conventional wisdom holds that only a "fool or a fiend" buys from vendors on the corner.[4]

Law enforcement, media, and policymakers alike claim that vertical business models dominate the street crack scene because it "serves their political, sensationalistic, and budgetary interests."[5] But these models do not, in fact, predominate. Monopolistic operations seemed to materialize only in New York and a few other cities. That they emerged at all, recognizing that they are ideal types, is a bit surprising given the tendency for lower-class street offenders to eschew subordination of any kind. Defiant, competitive, mistrustful, and Darwinistic, street offenders find it difficult to work within any organizational scheme, much less one requiring mutual obligation and hierarchical interdependence. Self-reliance takes precedence. Respect comes only with the demonstrated ability to be one's own boss.[6]

Whatever else one wants to say, selling crack—even in decline—is easy work. It requires little skill, start-up capital, or technical training. Sellers have no boss (at least, in the traditional sense of the term), no set hours, and, law enforcement aside, few formal constraints on their freedom. Participants make and implement their own decisions. The only schedule sellers have to meet is the one that they set. Effort and reward are conjoined in space and time, which has a tendency to offer perceptibly superior rewards. Although the $30 an hour reservation wage that once made it worth spending a year in prison for every two years spent dealing[7] no longer exists, sellers still can enjoy all the fruits of autonomy while "working." The risk of predation may be omnipresent, but it can be tempered to acceptable levels.

Undeniably, the rosy days of yesteryear have disappeared. Sellers who remain often compete intensely over a relatively small and largely indigent cadre of street addicts who constantly try to scam and bargain down prices. Crack selling may become a career choice by default, but even if we accept this, it continues to offer benefits and pleasures to its participants not available through other pursuits.

Indeed, to explain these offenders' behavior in strictly rational economic terms would miss the mark. The assumption that "all human behavior can be viewed as involving participants who maximize their utility from a stable set of preferences and accumulate an optimal amount of information and other inputs in a variety of markets"[8] ignores a panoply of subjective conditions that mediate individual choice. Selling illicit street drugs may represent one of the few remaining retail enterprises in which active agents can carve out their own freewheeling brand of entrepreneurship in a world overrun by bureaucratization.[9] The streets in general—and crack markets in particular—allow participants to "practice and display many virtues that cannot be practiced or displayed" elsewhere.[10] More than a source of material sustenance, selling crack may be one of the few meaningful arenas for the pursuit of prestige and self-worth available to a segment of the inner-city population. As calamitous as market conditions may be, the choice to sell is still quite functional for some. To abandon it for something else is either to forgo a source of accomplishment available nowhere else or, worse, to stare failure full in the face.[11]

Most offenders understand, however, that street crack selling is not a viable long-term vocation. A-Train thus claimed that he planned to stop selling "soon," insisting that slinging crack was "only for now. It's no life thing. I wanna own my own barber shop. I do this 'til I probly twenty or twenty-one [two more years]—'til I get me a car and save up some money." Double-D Loc, similarly, claimed that he would continue selling crack only until he was "halfway rich. I settle down in three or four years. Get me into a company." Yet these two and most of the others appeared to be doing nothing to get themselves to the point where they could successfully "retire." A number waxed responsible about husbanding resources, but the vast majority lived hand-to-mouth. Offenders did not save their dealing proceeds and had no bank accounts in which to deposit their funds. No offender claimed to invest his earnings in interest-bearing savings bonds or the stock market. Typically, they burned money as fast as they made it in the impulsive pursuit of hedonistic consumption.

Few sellers made a genuine attempt to move up the dealing chain and off the streetcorner. Theoretically, even the lowest-level pushers can do this by selling their inventory and using the proceeds to double their original wholesale purchase. "You buy a quarter [-ounce, for $250], sell that [for $500], then buy you a half-ounce, sell that [for $1,000], then buy you an ounce [and so on]," Fade explained. The strategy looks easy, but declining demand presents significant obstacles to its execution. The more product one has, the more difficulty one has in getting rid of it, and the more risk one assumes in doing so. Crack is not like fine wine. Its value does not increase with time; the only thing that grows is a seller's liability. Fade's experience is illustrative. After rising to the half-ounce point, he was locked up for twenty hours on a loitering violation. Much to his chagrin, on release he discovered that his stash had been unearthed by a resourceful group of crack-heads, who had found it under the board he had used to mark its location.

That curbside sellers lack the social capital for selling larger amounts—and the clientele who can afford to buy them—makes their prospects worse. The short-term cultivation tactics that offenders use to develop brand loyalty fail to address the fundamental issues that render their use necessary in the first place. Cultivation tactics also cannibalize a finite demand and induce other sellers to copy them—equalizing the playing field and making everyone worse off. Given the clientele to which such tactics are directed, they also may accelerate, or at least reinforce, the very stigmatization process that has caused crack's decline. That the dealing careers of most of these sellers "start at the bottom and proceed nowhere" is not surprising.[12]

ADAPTATION

Except for the fact that their product is both illicit and stigmatized, street crack sellers are no different from other entrepreneurial agents. Those who fail to evolve, adapt, and diversify are doomed. Thus, DuPont Chemical Corporation developed new product applications in response to evaporating post–World War II demand for explosives, the March of Dimes widened its focal breadth to include all birth defects rather than just polio when the Salk vaccine eliminated polio, and American universities began targeting the nontraditional student in the face of troublesome demographic shifts.[13] Few street crack sellers display such innovative responses to market changes.

Incredible though it may seem to some, evidence suggests that at least part of offenders' adaptation to a declining market ultimately may be absorption into the legal economy. In early 1998, the United States experienced its lowest unemployment levels in nearly thirty years. Teenage African American male unemployment reached a two-decade nadir. Two million new jobs were added in the last six months of 1997 alone, bringing the unemployment rate down to 4.7 percent, while the employment per population ratio reached a record high of 64.2 percent.[14] Persons once thought to be superfluous at best, or unemployable at worst, are being absorbed into the legal labor market where they often can earn wages in excess of the minimum. Previously important eligibility requirements—high school degree, prior job experience, clean arrest record—increasingly are being suspended in favor of putting warm bodies behind mops, brooms, stoves, counters, and (even) cash registers. As woefully unprepared for mainstream economic enterprise as these offenders may be, positions are being opened to them out of sheer necessity. Among the first to be absorbed undoubtedly will be those who would have been most likely to succeed in a declining streetcorner crack market.

Crime and legal work are not dichotomous choices, however; the line between the two is not a sharp one. Legal work and illegal work often go hand in hand as offenders "double up" on income sources or transition between the two.[15] Yet no matter how robust the economy, street-level crack sellers still lack one of the most fundamental prerequisites—sets of relationships with persons in positions of power and influence—that could allow them to make a *long-term transition* to legal income-producing activity. Permanent life change can occur only with the prudent accumulation of social capital.[16] The pervasive American myth that turning points in the life course can be realized if individuals just try hard enough is a "widely perpetrated fiction" rooted in the notion that individuals are the most important components in any society and that they have the free will to change their circumstances if they really want to.[17] Those who cannot adapt are failures—deficient individuals who deserve whatever fate befalls them.

Economies on the upswing certainly can jumpstart an individual's matrix of connections, but the charge may last only as long as the upswing itself. Both the cyclical nature of the U.S. economy and the trend toward labor deskilling and mechanization[18] suggest a bleak long-term outlook for most of these offenders. The more subjective problem is that offenders' "orientational stance" is in "direct contradiction to the humble, obedient modes of subservient social interaction" that are essential for successful participation in the legal economy—which only makes things worse.[19] Though it is reasonable to assume that an appreciable fraction of offenders will be absorbed into the legal economy, the absorption is likely to be partial, and many will continue to maintain strong ties to the street underworld. The worst of the worst inevitably remain, the persistent underclass "as omnipresent as potholes . . . [but] considerably more dangerous."[20]

THE NEXT CRACK?

If history is any indication, it is not a question of *if* a new drug will emerge onto this volatile scene but *when*—and what form it will take. The decline of one drug often signals the incubation of another.[21] Methamphetamine, widely discussed in drug enforcement and policy circles in the middle to late 1990s, reputedly is emerging as the nation's primary drug menace.[22] Perceptually, however, the drug has been linked to bikers and poor whites—limiting the breadth of its appeal. Meth also is too cheap and long-lasting a high to attract a massive influx of profit-minded vendors. A quarter-gram retails for around $25 and can produce a high that lasts twelve or more hours. This makes repetitive, binge usage unlikely. Psychedelics (such as LSD and MDMA) come and go, pulsating in miniepidemics that seem to coincide with Grateful Dead concerts and rave dances. MDMA ("ecstasy") received substantial media attention in the middle and late 1990s, but if national drug surveys are any indication, it is hype. Marijuana will persist as a kind of a vacuum filler when phase drugs like crack go out of style. Weed use has skyrocketed in the past five years and appears to be replacing crack as the drug of choice in urban areas across the country, especially among youth.[23] Nonetheless, the quantity required to get high, the nature and duration of that high, the drug's widespread availability, and its limited profit potential do not lend themselves to the McDonaldization crack experienced—nor to the systemic problems associated with crack.

One of the oldest, most established illicit street drugs—heroin—seems poised to make a comeback. Nationwide, the number of heroin addicts has been increasing since the 1970s, and growing numbers of teenagers and young adults report using the drug. In 1996 alone 141,000 new users were reported (up from 40,000 in 1992)—the majority of whom are under twenty-six years old. Heroin use among eighth-graders doubled in 1996, as did use by teenagers overall between 1991 and 1996, even while the use of other hard drugs declined. Emergency room "mentions" and treatment admissions for heroin in St. Louis, and across the country, have increased significantly. The number of heroin-related emergency room visits increased from 36,000 in 1991 to 76,000 in 1995, while the number of heroin-related deaths rose from

2,300 to 4,000. Though the overall incidence of drug-related emergency episodes decreased from a peak of 518,000 (1995) to 487,000 (1996), the decline can be traced primarily to five cities, and heroin-related admissions actually jumped 20 percent in the last two years of the study period.[24]

Relative to crack, heroin is thought to be a more sophisticated, sedating, safe, and controllable experience. Part of the reason for this perception lies in the high purity of the drug currently available at the retail level. National street heroin purity levels have risen considerably in recent years. In 1995, for example, the purity figure was nearly 40 percent nationwide, much higher than the 7 percent reported ten years ago. The quality of increasingly available South American heroin is even better—56.4 percent nationwide and 76 percent in New York City. Sixty-two percent of all U.S. heroin seizures since 1995 have involved South American–grown heroin, a seizure source figure that has doubled every year since 1993. Experimenters believe that they can sniff and snort this "new smack" in moderation without becoming addicted. Innovative marketing tactics such as small, snortable, concealable, and high-purity nickel-bag pick-me-ups are being targeted at inchoate suburban users and apparently are becoming quite popular. Moonrock, a crack and heroin amalgam with the addictive potential of cocaine and heroin combined, reportedly was being sold in New York in the middle to late 1990s. A smokable speedball, moonrock seems to have the concealability, heartiness, packaging flexibility, and marketing capacity once associated with retail crack.[25]

The implications of such trends could be far-reaching. Inevitably, the current high purity of street heroin will drop. Regardless of purity, studies unequivocally demonstrate that snorters and smokers rapidly become injectors. The specter of intravenous heroin use looms large with regard to AIDS. What is worse, injectors often engage in high-risk sexual behaviors, harbor perceptions of invincibility, and believe that even if they do become infected, protease inhibitors and combination drug therapy will cure them. This is to say nothing of the violence that accompanies drug markets during expansionary phases. Although the systemic, economic, and pharmacological factors that caused the explosion in predatory crime during the crack era are thought to be unparalleled, a number of conditions are in place for the cycle to repeat. Foremost among them are a sizable cadre of underemployed, financially needy, and strategically placed crack sellers; distribution networks delimited by territorial bounds; and the persistent availability of firearms. Whether these potentialities are realized or whether heroin's reincubation is bypassed in favor of some other yet unknown substance cannot be predicted with certainty.[26]

The enduring effect of crack's decline on illicit street economies is a related matter of considerable interest. The drugs-crime nexus is one of the most powerful and exhaustively studied relationships in all criminology. Decreases in drug use inevitably result in decreases in criminal behavior, and for crack, this relationship appears to be particularly strong. The most serious crime occurs among the heaviest crack users and includes offenses that extend beyond drug-related, income-generating activity and into the realm of revenge, racial antagonism, and the protection of image and honor. The marked reduction in violent crime starting in the early 1990s and continuing through the late 1990s—especially decreases in homicide rates—can be attributed directly to the market stabilization that came with the decline in crack usage. Given the sensitivity of violent crime rates to crack use, this downward trajectory is likely to persist.[27]

Fundamental changes in street capitalism both reinforce and amplify trends in the crack-violence connection. In the period between crack's incubation and decline, illicit street markets have been flooded with guns, jewelry, and consumer electronic goods. The bottom has dropped out of the price of once sought-after merchandise. This means less money for drugs, less time in dangerous places among high-risk persons, and less chance for violence to feed off property crimes. At the same time, methods of paying for commodities have undergone fundamental change. Between 1990 and 1994, credit card expenditures in the United States increased 57 percent to $731 billion. This "truly exponential" growth highlights a revolution in cash-avoidance behavior. Some have gone so far as to suggest that we are approaching a cashless society. Cash is street crime's lifeblood; without it, predatory crime (and the anomic pursuit of illicit street action that often gives rise to it) may begin to fade from the scene. That the attractiveness of cash as a commodity good to steal in its own right has dramatically increased in recent years is not surprising. The profound rise in robbery and decline in burglary rates between the mid-1980s and early 1990s attest to this. As the crack epidemic continues to abate, this trend is expected to ease as "the pressure to engage in violent property crime to generate quick cash is lessened." [28] Whether robbery and burglary resume their precrack patterns is open to question. Undoubtedly, offenders will develop other means for commodity transfer, whether through barter (sex has been used for the same purpose for quite some time now) or through illicit drugs themselves. In a cashless society, drugs may emerge as the new street currency, though how dealers will pay for their illegal importation remains a matter of speculation. [29]

CONCLUSION

Why crack never migrated outward to any great degree from central-city, predominantly African American neighborhoods is an intriguing issue but one that has received little attention. Obviously, a drug's euphoragenicity is neither racially nor socioeconomically determined. Drug preferences are linked to social status, and the experience of euphoria is to some degree socially constructed. Even so, crack's failure to radiate in a widespread and significant way is perplexing. We do know why it took hold. Inexpensive and widely available, crack became attractive to those who desired cocaine hydrochloride but could not afford it. CIA conspiracy theories and other fantastical claims aside, the process by which illicit drugs are identified with a specific population of acutely stigmatized users cannot be ignored. Such identification taints those drugs and mitigates their spread to other populations that believe the drugs to be foreign, uncouth, or uncool. Coupled with an undercurrent of racism, the results of such identification can be powerful, as crack attests: crack was the drug of choice in the inner city and nearly nowhere else. Supply-side factors only reinforced crack's central-city insularity. Street sellers typically lack the social capital that would allow unfettered expansion into suburban areas. This is to say nothing of the formal and informal social control mechanisms that would likely be triggered if the trade was taken there. Combined with the fear that suburban wannabe crack buyers often feel driving down to the ghetto—of arrest or victimization or both—crack's limited appeal may have been preordained from the start.

All of this is academic. Powerful anticrack norms have taken root in urban areas across the country that make *crack* a dirty word and vilify those who use it. Dramatic drops in consumption have been reported, especially among the youngest cohorts, who are most likely to persist as drug abusers well into their adult years. In New York City, once America's crack mecca, the number of eighteen- to twenty-year-olds who test positive for cocaine by urinalysis has dropped from 70 percent in 1986 to 21 percent in 1996; in Washington, D.C., from 64 percent in 1986 to 35 percent in 1996; and in Detroit, from 45 percent in 1987 to 5 percent in 1996. Though rates of positive urinalysis remain somewhat higher and are falling more slowly in St. Louis than in these other cities, significant reductions in this same cohort also have been demonstrated.[30] The epidemic is essentially over: demand for the substance has been siphoned off by stigma.

Clandestine use is the direction in which crack consumption is going. Users are sprinkling it into cigarettes and joints and are employing other less noxious means of delivery. Such methods distance users both physically and symbolically from the stigmatized category of crackhead.[31] These tactics may halt the plummeting rates of decline and may even lead to increased consumption if users view them as a nonstigmatizing, inexpensive way to get high without dire physical consequences. But there are no guarantees that street crack won't make a comeback. The cultural memory is short when it comes to drugs, and the specter of crack's reincubation inevitably looms. Heroin has developed a street cachet and romantic allure that stands in stark contrast to the lower-class, ghetto, nonglamorous drug image it once conjured. Though crack is unlikely ever to capture the same chic, it may be only a matter of time before its stigma begins to wear off. If or when this happens, it could be "déjà vu all over again" on the streetcorners of urban America.

Clearly, we understand a great deal about why crime in general and drug usage in particular incubate and expand; we know a lot less about why persons quit doing them both.[32] The idea that crack's decline was triggered largely by the efforts of law enforcement would be "comical if not for its underlying pathos."[33] Public policy has been more harmful and draconian than even the most disinterested of observers could have imagined.[34] Extraordinary numbers of crack market participants have been incapacitated, families broken apart, and communities destroyed. We should remember, however, that the drug's fall from grace was catalyzed first and foremost indigenously—that is, from within the street drug scene itself.

The crack experience can be profoundly pedagogical in this regard. Crack has highlighted and reinforced the indisputable power of stigma in directing human behavior. It is possible to manipulate stigma to beneficial ends. To say that image plays a prominent role in American society would be an understatement. Its importance in everyday interaction cannot be denied, nor can its role in selling everything from Pepsi to politicians. Image is especially important on the streets, particularly among drug users, where it offers the most important indicator of character. Perhaps more prudent and effective drug control policies can be developed through a "scarlet letter" approach. Strategies that tie image into negatively reinforcing, reintegrating messages, for example, may be able to trigger declines in future drug epidemics earlier and make them proceed faster. This is difficult, but it is not impossible. Drunk-driving labels on license plates and sex offender designation on drivers' permits represent two such attempts. The long-term success of such approaches, of course, is a bit murkier than many would care to admit. Scaring offenders straight by shocking or intimidating them may arouse fear and deter initially, but such policies almost inevitably fail in the end:[35] the harder authorities try to clamp down on something, the more attractive it often becomes. (The DARE program, Drug Abuse Resistance through Education, is the best and most recent example of this; children exposed to the drug use prevention program were more rather than less likely to use drugs later in adolescence.) The notion of reintegrating into normal society those who may have never been integrated in the first place is perhaps more vexing. To the extent that the use and distribution of illicit drugs are unresponsive to external influence, epidemics may largely be uncontrollable. The point is to address epidemics before they spin out of control so that the chronic social problems that give rise to them in the first place can be confronted and dealt with.

NOTES

CHAPTER 1

1. Dale D. Chitwood, James E. Rivers, and James A. Inciardi, *The American Pipe Dream: Crack Cocaine and the Inner City* (New York: Harcourt Brace, 1996).

2. Chitwood et al., *Pipe Dream*; on drug panics, see Erich Goode, *Drugs in American Society*, 3d ed. (New York: McGraw Hill, 1989); Bruce D. Johnson, Ansley Hamid, and Harry Sanabria, "Emerging Models of Crack Distribution," in Thomas Mieczkowski, ed., *Drugs and Crime: A Reader* (56–78) (Boston: Allyn and Bacon, 1992).

3. Constance Holden, "Streetwise Crack Research," *Science* 246 (1989): 1376–81; Bruce D. Johnson, Eloise Dunlap, Kathleen Boyle, and Bruce Jacobs, "Natural Transitions in Crack Distribution/Abuse," for National Institute on Drug Abuse (New York: National Drug Research Institute, 1997).

4. James A. Inciardi, Ruth Horowitz, and Anne E. Pottieger, *Street Kids, Street Drugs, Street Crime* (Belmont, Calif.: Wadsworth, 1993); Thomas Mieczkowski, "Crack Dealing on the Street: The Crew System and the Crack House," *Justice Quarterly* 9 (1992): 151–63.

5. In Philippe Bourgois, *In Search of Respect: Selling Crack in El Barrio* (Cambridge: Cambridge University Press, 1995), 80; on the pharmacology of crack cocaine, see also Philippe Bourgois and Eloise Dunlap, "Exorcising Sex-for-Crack in Harlem: An Ethnographic Perspective from Harlem," in Mitchell S. Ratner, ed., *Crack Pipe as Pimp: An Ethnographic Investigation of Sex-for-crack Exchanges* (97–132) (New York: Lexington, 1993), Chitwood et al., *Pipe Dream*, 12; Inciardi et al., *Street Kids*; David Ohlms, former president of the Greater St. Louis National Council on Drug and Alcohol Abuse, personal communication, 1997; but see Andrew Golub and Bruce D. Johnson, "Crack's Decline: Some Surprises across U.S. Cities," *Research in Brief* (p. 11) (Washington, D.C.: National Institute of Justice, 1997).

6. Bourgois, *In Search of Respect*, 75; see also Jeffrey Fagan, ed., Special Issue: Research on Crack, *Contemporary Drug Problems* 16(4) and 17(1) (1990).

7. G. Witkin, "The Men Who Created Crack," *U.S. News and World Report* (August 1991): 44–53; see also Bruce D. Johnson, "The Crack Era in New York City," *Addiction and Recovery* (May-June 1991): 24–27; Bruce D. Johnson, Andrew Golub, and Jeffrey Fagan, "Careers in Crack, Drug Use, Drug Distribution, and Nondrug Criminality," *Crime and Delinquency* 41 (1995): 281; Mieczkowski, "Crack Dealing."

8. On gangs and drug market instability, see Bourgois, *In Search of Respect*; Lisa Maher and Kathleen Daly, "Women in the Street-Level Drug Economy: Continuity or Change?" *Criminology* 34 (1996): 465–91; Chitwood et al., *Pipe Dream*; Scott H. Decker and Barrik Van Winkle, *Life in the Gang* (Cambridge: Cambridge University Press, 1996); on urban badlands, see Inciardi et al., *Street Kids*; Bruce D. Johnson, Terry Williams, Kojo A. Dei, and Harry Sanabria, "Drug Abuse in the Inner City: Impact on Hard Drug Users and the Community," in Michael Tonry and James Q. Wilson, eds., *Drugs and Crime* (Chicago: University of Chicago Press, 1990); Malcolm Klein, *The American Street Gang* (Oxford: Oxford University Press, 1995); Richard Rosenfeld, "The St. Louis Homicide Project: Local Responses to a National Problem," unpublished manuscript, 1991; Dan Waldorf, "Don't Be Your Own Best Customer: Drug Use of San Francisco Gang Drug Sellers," *Crime, Law, and Social Change* 19 (1993): 1–15; on social disorganization, see Robert J. Sampson, Stephen W. Raudenbush, and Felton Earls, "Neighborhoods and Violent Crime: A Multilevel Study of Collective Efficacy," *Science* 277 (1997): 918–24.

9. Cesar, "Younger Arrestees in U.S. Favor Marijuana; Older Arrestees Stay with Cocaine," *Cesar Fax*, vol. 6, issue 26, July 7 (1997); Drug Use Forecasting (DUF), *Annual Report* (Washington, D.C.: National Institute of Justice, 1996); Golub and Johnson, "Crack's Decline"; on the stigma of crack use, see Ansley Hamid, "The Developmental Cycle of a Drug Epidemic: The Cocaine Smoking Epidemic of 1981–1991," *Journal of Psychoactive Drugs* 24 (1992): 337–48; Thomas Mieczkowski, "Some Observations on the Scope of Crack Use and Distribution," in Thomas Mieczkowski, ed., *Drugs and Crime: A Reader* (32–55) (Boston: Allyn and Bacon, 1992).

10. Johnson et al., "Natural Transitions"; Office of National Drug Control Policy, "Pulse Check: National Trends in Drug Abuse" (Washington, D.C., 1996).

11. Cesar, "Younger Arrestees"; DUF, *Annual Report*; Office of National Drug Control Policy, Drugs and Crime Data (Washington, D.C., 1996).

12. Johnson et al., "Natural Transitions," 44.

13. See also Johnson et al., "Natural Transitions."

14. David Matza, *Delinquency and Drift* (Berkeley: University of California Press, 1969).

15. Richard A. Ball, "Sociology and General Systems Theory," *American*

Sociologist 13 (1978): 66; Walter Buckley, *Sociology and Modern Systems Theory* (Englewood Cliffs, N.J.: Prentice-Hall, 1967); Glenn B. Walters, *The Criminal Lifestyle* (Newbury Park, Calif.: Sage, 1990), 48.

16. Johnson et al., "Natural Transitions."

17. A. Mihalopoulos, "St. Louis County Loses Population for the First Time," *St. Louis Post Dispatch*, March 18, 1998, A1, A7; for more on urban decay, see William Julius Wilson, *The Truly Disadvantaged* (Chicago: University of Chicago Press, 1987); for urban decay in St. Louis, see Richard T. Wright and Scott H. Decker, *Burglars on the Job* (Boston: Northeastern University Press, 1994), 7.

18. See Federal Bureau of Investigation (FBI), *Uniform Crime Reports* (Washington, D.C.: U.S. Government Printing Office, 1994); Federal Bureau of Investigation (FBI), *Uniform Crime Reports* (Washington, D.C.: U.S. Government Printing Office, 1996); for St. Louis as research laboratory, see Richard Rosenfeld and Scott H. Decker, "Consent to Search and Seize: Evaluating an Innovative Youth Firearm Suppression Program," *Law and Contemporary Problems* 59 (1996): 197–219.

19. For epidemiological evidence, see DUF, *Annual Report*; Drug Abuse Warning Network (DAWN), "Preliminary Estimates of Drug-Related Emergency Department Episodes," Report 14 (Washington, D.C.: U.S. Department of Health and Human Services, 1996); for gangs and drugs in St. Louis, see Decker and Van Winkle, *Life in the Gang*; Heidi Israel and Jim Topolski, "Drug Trends in St. Louis" (St. Louis: Community Epidemiological Work Group, 1996).

20. Richard T. Wright and Scott H. Decker, *Armed Robbers in Action* (Boston: Northeastern University Press, 1997), 7; see also Inciardi et al., *Street Kids*, on urban dead zones.

21. George Rengert and J. Wasilchick, "Space, Time, and Crime: Ethnographic Insights into Residential Burglary," unpublished final report submitted to the U.S. Department of Justice, National Institute of Justice, 1990.

22. Hamid, "Developmental Cycle," 342.

23. Decker and Van Winkle, *Life in the Gang*; Fagan, "Special Issue"; Klein, *American Street Gang*; James F. Short Jr., *Poverty, Ethnicity, and Violent Crime* (Boulder: Westview, 1997); but see Felix M. Padilla, *The Gang as an American Enterprise* (New Brunswick, N.J.: Rutgers University Press, 1992); Martin Sanchez-Jankowski, *Islands in the Street* (Berkeley: University of California Press, 1991); Carl S. Taylor, *Dangerous Society* (East Lansing: Michigan State University Press, 1989).

24. Johnson et al., "Emerging Models"; see also Hamid, "Developmental Cycle"; Waldorf, "Best Customer."

25. Mark S. Fleisher, *Beggars and Thieves* (Madison: University of Wisconsin Press, 1995).

26. C. Bell and H. Newby, *Community Studies* (New York: Praeger, 1972), 1.

27. On the use of qualitative methods to study drug dealers, see, e.g., Patricia A. Adler, *Wheeling and Dealing* (New York: Columbia University Press, 1985); Michael Agar, *Ripping and Running: A Formal Ethnography of Urban Heroin Addicts* (New York: Seminar Press, 1973); Johnson et al., "Natural Transitions."

28. John Irwin, "Participant Observation of Criminals," in Jack Douglas, ed., *Research on Deviance* (New York: Random House, 1972), 117.

29. Agar, *Ripping and Running*, 25; Erich Goode, *The Marijuana Smokers* (New York: Basic Books, 1970); on other problems related to researching hard-to-reach populations, see Douglas D. Heckathorn, "Respondent-Driven Sampling: A New Approach to the Study of Hidden Populations," *Social Problems* 44 (1997): 174.

30. Jeffrey A. Sluka, "Participant Observation in Violent Social Contexts," *Human Organization* 49 (1990): 115.

31. Agar, *Ripping and Running*, 26.

32. Wright and Decker, *Burglars*, 5.

33. Edwin Sutherland and Donald Cressey, *Criminology*, 8th ed. (Philadelphia: Lippincott, 1970), 68.

34. Ned Polsky, *Hustlers, Beats, and Others* (Chicago: Aldine, 1967), 123.

35. George McCall, *Observing the Law* (New York: Free Press, 1978), 27; for more on the pitfalls of qualitative research with high-risk populations, see Adler, *Wheeling and Dealing*; Agar, *Ripping and Running*.

36. On hidden populations, see Marius Spreen, "Rare Populations, Hidden Populations, and Link-Tracing Designs: What and Why?" *Bulletin de Méthodologie Sociologique* 6 (1992): 34–58; J. K. Watters and Patrick Biernacki, "Targeted Sampling: Options for the Study of Hidden Populations," *Social Problems* 36 (1989): 416–30.

37. Erving Goffman, *Relations in Public: Micro Studies of the Public Order* (New York: Basic Books, 1971), 323.

38. Adler, *Wheeling and Dealing*; Elliot Liebow, *Tally's Corner* (Boston: Little, Brown, 1967).

39. Jeff Ferrell, "Criminological Verstehen: Inside the Immediacy of Crime," in Jeff Ferrell and Mark S. Hamm, eds., *Ethnography at the Edge: Crime, Deviance, and Field Research* (20–42) (Boston: Northeastern University Press, 1998).

40. Wright and Decker, *Burglars*, 28.

41. Polsky, *Hustlers*, 147.

42. Sluka, "Participant Observation."

43. See Erving Goffman, *Stigma: Notes on the Management of Spoiled Identity* (Englewood Cliffs, N.J.: Prentice-Hall, 1963).

44. John Van Maanen, "The Asshole," in Peter K. Manning and John Van Maanen, eds., *Policing: A View from the Street* (221–38) (Santa Monica: Goodyear, 1978).

45. Jerome H. Skolnick, *Justice without Trial* (New York: Wiley, 1966).

46. Jack D. Douglas, "Observing Deviance," in Jack D. Douglas, ed., *Research on Deviance* (3–34) (New York: Random House, 1972).

47. Sluka, "Participant Observation," 123.

48. Douglas, "Observing Deviance," 12.

49. James T. Carey, "Problems of Access and Risk in Observing Drug Scenes," in Jack D. Douglas, ed., *Research on Deviance* (77) (New York: Random House, 1972).

50. Polsky, *Hustlers*, 133–34; for more on legal issues in qualitative research, see Adler, *Wheeling and Dealing*, 24; Irving Soloway and James Walters, "Workin' the Corner: The Ethics and Legality of Fieldwork among Active Heroin Addicts," in Robert Weppner, ed., *Street Ethnography* (Beverly Hills: Sage, 1977).

51. See Jeffrey Fagan, "Drug Selling and Licit Income in Distressed Neighborhoods: The Economic Lives of Street-Level Drug Users and Dealers," in Adele V. Harrell and George E. Peterson, eds., *Drugs, Crime, and Social Isolation* (99–146) (Washington, D.C.: Urban Institute Press, 1991); Peter MacCoun and Peter Reuter, "Are the Wages of Sin $30 an Hour? Economic Aspects of Street-Level Drug Dealing," *Crime and Delinquency* 38 (1992): 477–91.

52. Laud Humphreys, *Tearoom Trade* (New York: Aldine de Gruyter, 1970); Thomas Mieczkowski, "'Geeking Up' and Throwing Down: Heroin Street Life in Detroit," *Criminology* 24 (1986): 645–66.

53. Barbara W. Lex, "Narcotics Addicts' Hustling Strategies: Creation and Manipulation of Ambiguity," *Journal of Contemporary Ethnography* 18 (1990): 393; for more on data collection using qualitative methods, see Agar, *Ripping and Running*; Wright and Decker, *Burglars*; Wright and Decker, *Armed Robbers*; James P. Spradley, *Participant Observation* (New York: Harcourt Brace, 1980).

54. Wright and Decker, *Burglars*, 26.

55. For more on these issues, see Richard A. Berk and Joseph M. Adams, "Establishing Rapport with Deviant Groups," *Social Problems* 18 (1970): 107; Polsky, *Hustlers*.

56. John Van Maanen, *Tales of the Field: On Writing Ethnography* (Chicago: University of Chicago Press, 1988), 56–57; see also Heckathorn, "Respondent-Driven Sampling," 179; Wright and Decker, *Burglars*, 23.

57. Fleisher, *Beggars and Thieves*, 80; on the reliability and validity of self-report data, see John C. Ball, "The Reliability and Validity of Interview Data Obtained from Fifty-nine Narcotic Drug Addicts," *American Journal of Sociology* 72 (1967): 650–54; Jan M. Chaiken and Marcia R. Chaiken, *Varieties of Criminal Behavior* (Santa Monica: Rand, 1982); Michael J. Hindelang, Travis Hirschi, and Joseph G. Weis, *Measuring Delinquency* (Beverly Hills: Sage, 1981); David Huizinga and Delbert Elliott, "Reassessing the Reliability and Validity of Self-Report Delinquency Measures," *Journal of Quantitative Criminology* 2 (1986): 293–327; Lisa Maher, *Sexed Work* (New York: Clarendon Press, 1997).

58. See James M. Henslin, "Studying Deviance in Four Settings: Research Experiences with Cabbies, Suicides, Drug Users, and Abortionees," in Jack Douglas, ed., *Research on Deviance* (52) (New York: Random House, 1972).

59. See, e.g., Bruce A. Jacobs, "Contingent Ties: Undercover Drug Officers' Use of Informants," *British Journal of Sociology* 48 (1997): 35–53; Bruce A. Jacobs, "Anticipatory Undercover Operations in High Schools," *Journal of Criminal Justice* 22 (1994): 445–57; Bruce A. Jacobs, "Undercover Deception Clues: A Case of Restrictive Deterrence," *Criminology* 31 (1993): 281–99.

60. Richard Wright and Michael Stein, "Seeing Ourselves: Exploring the Social Production of Criminological Knowledge in a Qualitative Methods Course," *Journal of Criminal Justice Education* 7 (1996): 66–77.

61. Heckathorn, "Respondent-Driven Sampling," 114; for more on external validity, see Barry Glassner and Cheryl Carpenter, "The Feasibility of an Ethnographic Study of Property Offenders: A Report Prepared for the National Institute of Justice" (Washington, D.C.: National Institute of Justice, mimeo, 1985); Wright and Decker, *Burglars*, 21.

62. See, e.g., Kathleen Boyle and M. Douglas Anglin, "'To the Curb': Sex Bartering and Drug Use among Homeless Crack Users in Los Angeles," in Mitchell S. Ratner, ed., *Crack Pipe as Pimp: An Ethnographic Investigation of Sex-for-Crack Exchanges* (159–86) (New York: Lexington, 1993); Chitwood et al., *Pipe Dream*; Johnson et al., "Crack Era in New York City"; Lawrence Oullet, J. W. Wayne Wiebel, Antonio Jimenez, and Wendell A. Johnson, "Crack Cocaine and the Transformation of Prostitution in Three Chicago Neighborhoods," in Mitchell S. Ratner, ed., *Crack Pipe as Pimp: An Ethnographic Investigation of Sex-for-Crack Exchanges* (69–96) (New York: Lexington, 1993).

63. Johnson et al., "Natural Transitions"; but see John M. Hagedorn, *People and Folks* (Chicago: Lake View Press, 1988); Mieczkowski, "'Geeking Up' and Throwing Down."

64. Wright and Decker, *Armed Robbers*, 31.

65. See also Robert Prus, "Purchasing Products for Resale: Assessing Suppliers as 'Partners-in-Trade'," *Symbolic Interaction* 7 (1984): 253.

CHAPTER 2

1. Eloise Dunlap and Bruce D. Johnson, "The Setting for the Crack Era: Macro Forces, Micro Consequences," *Journal of Psychoactive Drugs* 24 (1992): 307–21; Johnson et al., "Natural Transitions"; on poverty and social disorganization, see Robert J. Sampson, Stephen W. Raudenbush, and Felton Earls, "Neighborhoods and Violent Crime: A Multilevel Study of Collective Efficacy," *Science* 277 (1997): 918–24; William Julius Wilson, *When Work Disappears* (New York: Knopf, 1996).

2. John Lofland, *Deviance and Identity* (Englewood Cliffs, N.J.: Prentice-Hall, 1969).

3. Bourgois, *In Search of Respect*, 83; Johnson et al., "Drug Abuse in the Inner City"; Peter MacCoun and Peter Reuter, "Are the Wages of Sin $30 an Hour? Economic Aspects of Street-Level Drug Dealing," *Crime and Delinquency* 38 (1992): 477–91.

4. Bourgois, *In Search of Respect*; Fleisher, *Beggars and Thieves*, 197.

5. E. F. Loftus, "Memory and its Distortions," in A. G. Kraut, ed., *G. Stanley Hall Lectures* (119–54) (Washington, D.C.: American Psychological Association, 1982), 146; M. Ross, "Relation of Implicit Theories to the Construction of Personal Histories," *Psychological Review* 96 (1989): 341–57.

6. MacCoun and Reuter, "Wages," 488.

7. Cf. Charles Jaco, KMOX Radio Telecast, St. Louis, Mo., Winter 1997.

8. Pierre Bourdieu, *Distinction*, trans. Richard Nice (Cambridge: Harvard University Press, 1984).

9. Fleisher, *Beggars and Thieves*, 145.

10. Walters, *Criminal Lifestyle*, 73; see also Jan M. Chaiken and Marcia R. Chaiken, *Varieties of Criminal Behavior* (Santa Monica: Rand, 1982).

11. Wright and Decker, *Armed Robbers*, 39–46.

12. Dermot Walsh, "Victim Selection Procedures among Economic Criminals: The Rational Choice Perspective," in Derek Cornish and Ronald Clarke, eds., *The Reasoning Criminal: Rational Choice Perspectives on Offending* (40–52) (New York: Springer-Verlag, 1986).

13. Jack Katz, *Seductions of Crime: Moral and Sensual Attractions in Doing Evil* (New York: Basic Books, 1988).

14. Wright and Decker, *Armed Robbers*, 40.

15. Erving Goffman, *Stigma: Notes on the Management of Spoiled Identity* (Englewood Cliffs, N.J.: Prentice-Hall, 1963).

16. Wright and Decker, *Armed Robbers*, 41.

17. Bourgois, *In Search of Respect*, 158.

18. Neal Shover and David Honaker, "The Socially Bounded Decision Making of Persistent Property Offenders," *Howard Journal of Criminal Justice* 31 (1992): 276–93; Walters, *The Criminal Lifestyle*; Wright and Decker, *Burglars*.

19. Neal Shover, *Great Pretenders* (Boulder: Westview, 1996), 104; Walters, *Criminal Lifestyle*, 147.

20. See also Elijah Anderson, *Streetwise* (Chicago: University of Chicago Press, 1990).

21. See Bourgois, *In Search of Respect*.

22. Johnson et al., "Drug Abuse" 47.

23. Johnson et al., "Drug Abuse."

24. Georg Simmel, "A Chapter in the Philosophy of Money," *American Journal of Sociology* 5 (1900): 577–603.

25. Bourgois, *In Search of Respect*, 91.

26. Bourgois, *In Search of Respect*, 115; Walter B. Miller, "Lower-Class Culture as a Generating Milieu of Gang Delinquency," *Journal of Social Issues* 14 (1958): 12.

27. Walters, *Criminal Lifestyle*, 88, 93.

28. Walters, *Criminal Lifestyle*, 93.

29. Howard Finestone, *Cats, Kicks, and Color* (New York: Free Press, 1957), 284; see also Richard Dembo, Linda Williams, Werner Wothke, James Schmeidler, Alan Getreu, Estellita Berry, Eric D. Wish, and Candace Christiansen, "The Relationship between Cocaine Use, Drug Sales, and Other Delinquency among a Cohort of High-Risk Youths Over Time," in M. De La Rosa, E. Y. Lambert, and B. Gropper, eds., *Drugs and Violence: Causes, Correlates, and Consequences* (112–35) (Rockville, Md.: National Institute on Drug Abuse, 1990); Paul J. Goldstein, "Getting Over: Economic Alternatives to Predatory Crime among Street Drug Users," in James A. Inciardi, ed., *The Drug-Crime Connection* (67–84) (Beverly Hills: Sage, 1981); see also Inciardi et al., *Street Kids*; Edward Preble and John J. Casey, "Taking Care of Business: The Heroin User's Life on the Street," *International Journal of the Addictions* 4 (1969): 1–24.

30. Bourgois, *In Search of Respect*.

31. See also Bourgois, *In Search of Respect*, 77, 93.

32. Jeffrey Fagan and Ko-lin Chin, "Initiation into Crack and Cocaine: A Tale of Two Epidemics," *Contemporary Drug Problems* 16 (1989): 579–618; Inciardi et al., *Street Kids*.

33. On the addiction liability of crack cocaine, see Bourgois and Dunlap, "Exorcising Sex-for-Crack in Harlem"; James A. Inciardi, D. Lockwood, and Annie E. Pottieger, *Women and Crack Cocaine* (New York: Macmillan, 1993); Thomas Mieczkowski, "Crack Distribution in Detroit," *Contemporary Drug Problems* (1990) 17: 27.

34. Shover and Honaker, "Socially Bounded Decision Making," 289.

35. R. Dawkins, *The Blind Watchmaker* (Harlow: Longman, 1986), 302.

36. Bourgois, *In Search of Respect*, 85; Terry Furst, "The Stigmatized Image of the Crackhead," unpublished manuscript, NDRI, New York, 1995, 14; Johnson et al., "Natural Transitions."

37. See Cheryl Carpenter, Barry Glassner, Bruce D. Johnson, and Julia Loughlin, *Kids, Drugs, and Crime* (Lexington, Mass.: Lexington Books, 1988); Decker and Van Winkle, *Life in the Gang*; Malcolm W. Klein, *Street Gangs and Street Workers* (Englewood Cliffs, N.J.: Prentice-Hall, 1971); Joan W. Moore, *Homeboys: Gangs, Drugs, and Prisons in the Barrios of Los Angeles* (Philadelphia: Temple University Press, 1978); Felix M. Padilla, *The Gang as an American Enterprise* (New Brunswick, N.J.: Rutgers University Press, 1992); Sanchez-Jankowski, *Islands in the Street*; James F. Short Jr. and Fred L. Strodtbeck, *Group Process and Gang Delinquency* (Chicago: University of Chicago Press, 1965); Frederic Thrasher, *The Gang: A Study of 1313 Gangs in Chicago* (Chicago: University of Chicago Press, 1928); James Diego Vigil, *Barrio Gangs: Street Life and Identity in Southern California* (Austin: University of Texas Press, 1988); Franklin E. Zimring, "Kids, Groups, and

Crime: Some Implications of a Well-Known Secret," *Journal of Criminal Law and Criminology* 72 (1981): 867–85.

38. Drug Use Forecasting (DUF), *Quarterly Report* (Washington, D.C.: National Institute of Justice, 1997).

39. Cesar, "Marijuana Replacing Cocaine as Drug of Choice among Adult Arrestees," *Cesar Fax*, vol. 6, issue 25, June 30 (1997).

40. Andrew Hathaway, "Marijuana and Lifestyle: Exploring Tolerable Deviance," *Deviant Behavior* 18 (1997): 213–32; but see National Institute on Drug Abuse, Agency statement, March 31, 1998.

41. For marijuana, see Allen B. Fields, "Slinging Weed: The Social Organization of Streetcorner Marijuana Sales," *Urban Life* 13 (1984): 247–70; for cocaine powder, see Adler, *Wheeling and Dealing*; for heroin, see Edward Preble and John J. Casey, "Taking Care of Business: The Heroin User's Life on the Street," *International Journal of the Addictions* 4 (1969): 1–24; but see Mieczkowski, "'Geeking Up' and Throwing Down"; for crack, see Johnson et al., "Emerging Models of Crack Distribution."

42. Bruce D. Johnson, Paul Goldstein, Edward Preble, James Schmeidler, Douglas S. Lipton, Barry Spunt, and Thomas Miller, *Taking Care of Business: The Economics of Crime by Heroin Abusers* (Lexington, Mass.: Lexington Books, 1985).

43. E. P. Deschenes and P. W. Greenwood, "Treating the Juvenile Offender," *Journal of Contemporary Criminology* 9 (1993): 146–67; Peter Reuter, Robert MacCoun, and Patrick Murphy, *Money from Crime* (Santa Monica: Rand, 1990).

44. Fagan and Chin, "Initiation into Crack and Cocaine."

45. Jerome H. Skolnick, Theodore Correl, Elizabeth Navarro, and Roger Rabb, "The Social Structure of Street Drug Dealing," in Larry K. Gaines and Peter B. Kraska, eds., *Drugs, Crime, and Justice* (159–91) (Prospect Heights, Ill.: Waveland Press, 1997); on the prohibitions against drug use in gangs, see also Decker and Van Winkle, *Life in the Gang*; Sanchez-Jankowski, *Islands in the Street*; Waldorf, "Don't Be Your Own Best Customer"; for survey data on youthful drug using patterns, see Jerald G. Bachman, Lloyd D. Johnston, and Patrick O'Malley, "Monitoring the Future: Questionnaire Responses from the Nation's High School Seniors" (Ann Arbor, Mich.: Institute for Social Research at the University of Michigan, 1981); Delbert S. Elliott, David Huizinga, and Suzanne Ageton, *Explaining Delinquency and Drug Use* (Beverly Hills: Sage, 1985).

46. Wright and Decker, *Burglars*, 54.

47. Lofland, *Deviance and Identity*.

48. Shover and Honaker, "Socially Bounded Decision Making," 283.

49. Shover, *Great Pretenders*.

50. Stephen Baron and Timothy Hartnagel, "Attributions, Affect, and Crime: Street Youths' Reactions to Unemployment," *Criminology* 35 (1997): 409–34.

51. John Hagan and Bill McCarthy, *Mean Streets: Youth Crime and Homelessness* (New York: Cambridge University Press, 1997).

CHAPTER 3

1. Neal Shover, "Tarnished Goods in the Marketplace," *Urban Life and Culture* 3 (1975): 471–88.

2. See also Mieczkowski, "Crack Dealing on the Street," 157; Johnson et al., "Emerging Models"; Shover, "Tarnished Goods."

3. Johnson et al., "Emerging Models," 65.

4. See Decker and Van Winkle, *Life in the Gang*; Klein, *American Street Gang*.

5. Prus, "Purchasing Products," 250.

6. Marvin B. Scott, *The Racing Game* (Chicago: Aldine, 1968).

7. Johnson et al., "Emerging Models."

8. Sanchez-Jankowski, *Islands in the Street.*

9. Neal Shover and David Honaker, "The Socially Bounded Decision Making of Persistent Property Offenders," *Howard Journal of Criminal Justice* 31 (1992): 276–93.

10. Chitwood, Rivers, and Inciardi, *The American Pipe Dream*, 11.

11. Prus, "Purchasing Products," 256.

12. James A. Inciardi, "Kingrats, Chicken Heads, Slow Necks, Freaks, and Blood Suckers: A Glimpse at the Miami Sex-for-Crack Market," in Mitchell S. Ratner, ed., *Crack Pipe as Pimp* (37–67) (New York: Lexington Books, 1993).

13. Philippe Bourgois, Mark Lettiere, and James Quesada, "Social Misery and the Sanctions of Substance Abuse: Confronting HIV Risk among Homeless Heroin Addicts in San Francisco," *Social Problems* 44 (1997): 162–63.

14. Prus, "Purchasing Products," 259.

15. Prus, "Purchasing Products."

16. See, e.g., Decker and Van Winkle, *Life in the Gang*; Waldorf, "Don't Be Your Own Best Customer."

17. LaMar T. Empey and Mark C. Stafford, *American Delinquency* (Belmont: Wadsworth, 1991), 243; see also Klein, *The American Street Gang*; Walter B. Miller, "Lower-Class Culture as a Generating Milieu of Gang Delinquency," *Journal of Social Issues* 14 (1958): 5–19; Short and Strodtbeck, *Group Process and Gang Delinquency.*

18. Decker and Van Winkle, *Life in the Gang*, 162.

19. Georg Simmel, "The Stranger," in Donald Levine, ed., *Georg Simmel* (143–49) (Chicago: University of Chicago Press, 1908).

20. Stanford Lyman, *The Seven Deadly Sins* (Dix Hills, N.Y.: General Hall, 1989), 55; Peter K. Manning, *The Narcs' Game* (Cambridge: MIT Press, 1980).

21. Waldorf, "Don't Be Your Own Best Customer," 6.

22. Johnson et al., "Emerging Models," 62.

23. Peter MacCoun and Peter Reuter, "Are the Wages of Sin $30 an Hour? Economic Aspects of Street-Level Drug Dealing, " *Crime and Delinquency* 38 (1992): 489.

24. Fleisher, *Beggars and Thieves*, 186.

25. Patricia Brantingham and Paul Brantingham, "Criminality of Place: Crime Generators and Crime Attractors," *European Journal on Crime Policy and Research*, Special Issue on Crime, Environment, and Situational Prevention 3 (1995): 1–19.

26. Odis E. Bigus, "The Milkman and His Customer: A Cultivated Relationship," *Urban Life and Culture* 1 (1972): 131.

27. See, e.g., Adler, *Wheeling and Dealing*; Bigus, "The Milkman"; Robert Prus, "Developing Loyalty: Fostering Purchasing Relationships in the Marketplace," *Urban Life* 15 (1987): 331–66.

28. Prus, "Purchasing Products," 261.

29. Agar, *Ripping and Running*, 89–90.

30. Bigus, "The Milkman."

31. Barbara W. Lex, "Narcotics Addicts' Hustling Strategies: Creation and Manipulation of Ambiguity," *Journal of Contemporary Ethnography* 18 (1990): 388–415.

32. See also Prus, "Purchasing Products," 259.

33. Skolnick et al., "The Social Structure of Street Drug Dealing."

34. Bigus, "The Milkman."

35. Decker and Van Winkle, *Life in the Gang*, 168.

36. Walters, *Criminal Lifestyle*, 132.

37. See Shover, "Tarnished Goods."

38. Shover, *Great Pretenders*.

39. Fagan, "Drug Selling and Licit Income," 117.

40. Skolnick et al., "The Social Structure of Street Drug Dealing," 174.

41. N. Curcione, "Suburban Snowmen: Facilitating Factors in the Careers of Middle-Class Coke Dealers," *Deviant Behavior* 18 (1997): 249.

42. Decker and Van Winkle, *Life in the Gang*, 17.

43. K. Jack Riley, "Homicide and Drugs: A Tale of Six Cities," *Homicide Studies* 2 (1998): 195.

44. But see Riley, "Homicide and Drugs," 195.

45. See Prus, "Developing Loyalty."

CHAPTER 4

1. Patricia Brantingham and Paul Brantingham, "Criminality of Place: Crime Generators and Crime Attractors," *European Journal on Crime Policy and Research*, Special Issue on Crime, Environment, and Situational Prevention 3 (1995): 1; see also Bruce D. Johnson, Paul Goldstein, Edward Preble, James Schmeidler, Douglas S. Lipton, Barry Spunt, and Thomas Miller, *Taking Care of Business: The Economics of Crime by Heroin Abusers* (Lexington, Mass.: Lexington Books, 1985), 177.

2. Federal Bureau of Investigation (FBI), *Uniform Crime Reports* (Washington, D.C.: U.S. Government Printing Office, 1993); Rosenfeld, "St. Louis Homicide Project."

3. Paul J. Goldstein, "The Drugs/Violence Nexus: A Tripartite Conceptual Framework," *Journal of Drug Issues* 15 (1985): 493–506.

4. K. Jack Riley, *Crack, Powder, and Heroin: Drug Use and Purchase Patterns in Six U.S. Cities* (Washington, D.C.: National Institute of Justice and the Office of National Drug Control Policy, 1997).

5. K. Jack Riley, "Homicide and Drugs: A Tale of Six Cities," *Homicide Studies* 2 (1998): 176–205.

6. For a full discussion of these issues, see Alfred Blumstein and Richard Rosenfeld, "Explaining Recent Trends in U.S. Homicide Rates," *Journal of Criminology and Criminal Law* (1998); Riley, "Homicide and Drugs."

7. Philippe Bourgois, Mark Lettiere, and James Quesada, "Social Misery and the Sanctions of Substance Abuse: Confronting HIV Risk among Homeless Heroin Addicts in San Francisco," *Social Problems* 44 (1997): 164; for more on hustling and getting over, see John C. Ball, John W. Shaffer, and David N. Nurco, "The Day-to-Day Criminality of Heroin Addicts in Baltimore: A Study in the Continuity of Offense Rates," *Drug and Alcohol Dependence* 12 (1983): 119–42; Chitwood, Rivers, and Inciardi, *The American Pipe Dream*, 40; Allen Fields and James M. Walters, "Hustling: Supporting a Heroin Habit," in B. Hanson, G. Beschner, J. M. Walters, and E. Bovelle, eds., *Life with Heroin: Voices from the Inner City* (Lexington, Mass.: Lexington Books, 1985); Paul J. Goldstein, "Getting Over: Economic Alternatives to Predatory Crime among Street Drug Users," in James A. Inciardi, ed., *The Drug-Crime Connection* (67–84) (Beverly Hills: Sage, 1981).

8. Agar, *Ripping and Running*, 61.

9. Fleisher, *Beggars and Thieves*, 44.

10. See Agar, *Ripping and Running*, 46.

11. Hamid, "The Developmental Cycle of a Drug Epidemic."

12. See Johnson et al., *Taking Care of Business*, 177.

13. Agar, *Ripping and Running*, 52; Mieczkowski, "Crack Dealing on the Street," 157.

14. C. Wright Mills, "Situated Actions and Vocabularies of Motive," *American Sociological Review* 5 (1940): 904.

15. See Fleisher, *Beggars and Thieves*; Bruce A. Jacobs, "Drug Dealing and Negative Reciprocity," *Deviant Behavior* 19 (1998): 29–49.

16. Michael W. Macy and Andreas Flache, "Beyond Rationality in Models of Choice," *Annual Review of Sociology* 21 (1995): 87; on burning customers, see Agar, *Ripping and Running*; Mieczkowski, "'Geeking Up' and Throwing Down," 653; on self-enclosed cycles of reinforcing behaviors, see Edwin Lemert, "An Isolation and Closure Theory of Naive Check Forgery," *Journal of Criminal Law, Criminology, and Police Science* 44 (1953): 296–307.

17. Fleisher, *Beggars and Thieves*, 160.

18. See Janet L. Lauritsen, Robert J. Sampson, and John H. Laub, "The Link between Offending and Victimization among Adolescents," *Criminology* 29 (1991): 265–91; Richard F. Sparks, *Research on Victims of Crime* (Washington, D.C.: U.S. Government Printing Office, 1982).

19. For a complete discussion of this and related issues, see Wright and Decker, *Armed Robbers*, 42.

20. For violence and drug dealing, see Fagan, "Drug Selling and Licit Income," 115; Goldstein, "The Drugs/Violence Nexus;" Rosenfeld, "The St. Louis Homicide Project"; Terry Williams, Eloise Dunlap, Bruce D. Johnson, and Ansley Hamid, "Personal Safety in Dangerous Places," *Journal of Contemporary Ethnography* 21 (1992): 343–74; for target familiarity, see Wright and Decker, *Armed Robbers*.

21. Wright and Decker, *Armed Robbers*, 98.

22. See Wright and Decker, *Armed Robbers*, 102–03; on copresence, see Erving Goffman, *Relations in Public: Micro Studies of the Public Order* (New York: Basic Books, 1971).

23. See Williams et al., "Personal Safety."

24. See also Bourgois, *In Search of Respect*.

25. Carolyn Phillipps, Research Liaison, St. Louis City Police Department, personal communication, October 10, 1997.

26. Lauritsen et al., "Offending and Victimization," 268.

27. Lisa Maher, *Sexed Work* (New York: Clarendon Press, 1997).

28. Johnson et al., *Taking Care of Business*, 172, 174; also see Wright and Decker, *Armed Robbers*.

29. Maher and Daly, "Women in the Street-Level Drug Economy," 483.

30. Bourgois, *In Search of Respect*, 88.

31. Elijah Anderson, *Streetwise* (Chicago: University of Chicago Press, 1990).

32. Wright and Decker, *Armed Robbers*, 67.

33. See also Wright and Decker, *Armed Robbers*.

34. See Bourgois, *In Search of Respect*; Johnson et al., *Taking Care of Business*.

35. On the collective conscience, see Emile Durkheim, *The Division of Labor in Society* (New York: Free Press, 1964); on the mentality of gang members and drug sellers, see Mieczkowski, "'Geeking Up' and Throwing Down," 658; Klein, *American Street Gang*.

CHAPTER 5

1. A. Mark, R. Kleiman, and K. D. Smith, "State and Local Drug Enforcement: In Search of a Strategy," in Michael Tonry and James Q. Wilson, eds., *Drugs and Crime* (vol. 13, pp. 69–108) (Chicago: University of Chicago Press, 1990), 85.

2. See Chitwood, Rivers, and Inciardi, *The American Pipe Dream*, 50.

3. Office of National Drug Control Policy, *National Drug Control Strategy* (Washington, D.C.: White House, 1990), 3.

4. See Erving Goffman, *Relations in Public: Micro Studies of the Public Order* (New York: Basic Books, 1971), 242; Erving Goffman, *Stigma: Notes on the Management of Spoiled Identity* (Englewood Cliffs, N.J.: Prentice-Hall, 1963), 88.

5. See also Allen B. Fields, "Slinging Weed: The Social Organization of Streetcorner Marijuana Sales," *Urban Life* 13: 264.

6. See also Bruce D. Johnson and Mangai Natarajan, "Strategies to Avoid Arrest: Crack Sellers' Response to Intensified Policing," *American Journal of Police* 14 (1995): 59.

7. See Laud Humphreys, *Tearoom Trade* (New York: de Gruyter, 1970).

8. Goffman, *Stigma*, 97.

9. Alfred Schutz, *The Phenomenology of the Social World* (Evanston, Ill.: Northwestern University Press, 1967).

10. See also Fleisher, *Beggars and Thieves*, 129.

11. Humphreys, *Tearoom Trade*, 12.

12. Humphreys, *Tearoom Trade*, 166.

13. Scott Feld, "The Focused Organization of Social Ties," *American Journal of Sociology* 86 (1981): 1015–35.

14. See Jerome H. Skolnick, *Justice without Trial* (New York: Wiley, 1966).

15. See Erving Goffman, *Presentation of Self in Everyday Life* (Garden City, N.Y.: Anchor, 1959).

16. Goffman, *Stigma*, 102.

17. See Mieczkowski, "'Geeking Up' and Throwing Down," 652.

18. See LaMar T. Empey and Mark C. Stafford, *American Delinquency* (Belmont: Wadsworth, 1991); Malcolm Klein and L. Y. Crawford, "Groups, Gangs, and Cohesiveness," in James F. Short Jr., ed., *Gang Delinquency and Delinquency Subcultures* (New York: Harper & Row, 1967).

19. For drug dealing as an economic activity, see Peter Reuter and M. A. R. Kleiman, "Risk and Prices: An Economic Analysis of Drug Enforcement," in Michael Tonry and Norval Morris, eds., *Crime and Justice: An Annual Review of Research* (vol. 7) (Chicago: University of Chicago Press, 1986); for nondisruptive arrest-avoidance strategies, see Johnson and Natarajan, "Strategies to Avoid Arrest," 50.

20. Robert E. Worden, Timothy S. Bynum, and J. Frank, "Police Crackdowns on Drug Abuse and Trafficking," in D. L. MacKenzie and Craig D. Uchida, eds., *Drugs and Crime* (95–113) (Thousand Oaks, Calif.: Sage, 1994), 96.

21. Kevin Ryan, "Technicians and Interpreters in Moral Crusaders: The Case of the Drug Courier Profile," *Deviant Behavior* 15 (1994): 226.

22. See Fleisher, *Beggars and Thieves*; Shover, *Great Pretenders*; Wright and Decker, *Burglars on the Job*.

23. See, e.g., John C. Ball, John W. Shaffer, and David N. Nurco, "The Day-to-Day Criminality of Heroin Addicts in Baltimore: A Study in the Continuity of Offense Rates," *Drug and Alcohol Dependence* 12 (1983): 119–42.

24. Bruce D. Johnson, Paul Goldstein, Edward Preble, James Schmeidler, Douglas S. Lipton, Barry Spunt, and Thomas Miller, *Taking Care of Business: The Economics of Crime by Heroin Abusers* (Lexington, Mass.: Lexington Books, 1985).

25. James A. Inciardi, *Heroin Use and Street Crime* (Los Angeles: Roxbury, 1995).

26. See Fleisher, *Beggars and Thieves*, on jails as sanctuaries.

27. See Neal Shover, *Great Pretenders* (Boulder: Westview, 1996).

28. Johnson and Natarajan, "Strategies to Avoid Arrest."

29. See also Mieczkowski, "'Geeking Up' and Throwing Down," 652.

30. W. William Minor and Joseph Harry, "Deterrent and Experiential Effects in Perceptual Deterrence Research: A Replication and Extension," *Journal of Research in Crime and Delinquency* 19 (1982): 190–203.

CHAPTER 6

1. Mieczkowski, "'Geeking Up' and Throwing Down," 651; see also Adler, *Wheeling and Dealing*; Bourgois, *In Search of Respect*; James T. Carey, *The College Drug Scene* (Englewood Cliffs, N.J.: Prentice-Hall, 1968); Allen B. Fields, "Slinging Weed: The Social Organization of Streetcorner Marijuana Sales," *Urban Life* 13 (1984): 247–70; Johnson and Natarajan, "Strategies to Avoid Arrest"; John Langer, "Drug Entrepreneurs and Dealing Culture," *Social Problems* 24 (1976): 377–85.

2. See Erich Goode, *The Marijuana Smokers* (New York: Basic Books, 1970).

3. See also Johnson and Natarajan, "Strategies to Avoid Arrest," 53.

4. See also Erving Goffman, *Relations in Public: Micro Studies of the Public Order* (New York: Basic Books, 1971), 246.

5. Laud Humphreys, *Tearoom Trade* (New York: Aldine de Gruyter, 1970), 59.

6. Simmel in Erving Goffman, *Stigma: Notes on the Management of Spoiled Identity* (Englewood Cliffs, N.J.: Prentice-Hall, 1963), 93.

7. Jerome H. Skolnick, *Justice without Trial* (New York: Wiley, 1966).

8. Inciardi, "Kingrats."

9. In Decker and Van Winkle, *Life in the Gang*, 168.

10. Johnson and Natarajan, "Strategies to Avoid Arrest," 58.

11. M. Sviridoff and Sally T. Hillsman, "Assessing the Community Effects of Tactical Narcotics Teams," in D. L. MacKenzie and Craig D. Uchida, eds., *Drugs and Crime* (114–28) (Thousand Oaks, Calif.: Sage, 1994), 120.

12. Elijah Anderson, *Streetwise* (Chicago: University of Chicago Press, 1990), 169.

13. Goffman, *Relations in Public*, 210.

14. Bruce A. Jacobs, "Undercover Deception Clues: A Case of Restrictive Deterrence," *Criminology* 31 (1993): 281–99.

15. See Henry Brownstein, *The Rise and Fall of a Violent Crime Wave* (New York: Harrow and Heston, 1996).

16. Emile Durkheim, *Suicide* (New York: Free Press, 1951).

17. Jack P. Gibbs, *Crime, Punishment, and Deterrence* (New York: Elsevier, 1975), 33.

18. Gibbs, *Crime, Punishment, and Deterrence*, 33.

19. See also Sheldon Ekland-Olson, John Lieb, and Louis Zurcher, "The Paradoxical Impact of Criminal Sanctions: Some Microstructural Findings," *Law and Society Review* 18 (1984): 165.

20. Charles R. Tittle, *Sanctions and Social Deviance: The Question of Deterrence* (New York: Praeger, 1980).

21. Ernest van den Haag, *Punishing Criminals: Concerning a Very Old and Basic Question* (New York: Basic Books, 1975).

22. Edwin Schur, *Labeling Deviant Behavior: Its Sociological Implications* (New York: Harper & Row, 1971), 69–81.

23. Ekland-Olson et al., "Paradoxical Impact."

24. See National Institute of Justice, *Quarterly Briefing* (Washington, D.C.: U.S. Government Printing Office, 1998).

25. Peter Letkemann, *Crime as Work* (Englewood Cliffs, N.J.: Prentice-Hall, 1973), 143.

26. See Trevor Bennett and Richard Wright, *Burglars on Burglary: Prevention and the Offender* (Aldershot, U.K.: Gower, 1984); Floyd Feeney, "Robbers as Decision-Makers," in Derek Cornish and Ronald Clarke, eds., *The Reasoning Criminal: Rational Choice Perspectives on Offending* (53–71) (New York: Springer-Verlag, 1986); Kenneth D. Tunnell, *Choosing Crime: The Criminal Calculus of Property Offenders* (Chicago: Nelson-Hall Publishers, 1992); Wright and Decker, *Burglars on the Job.*

27. Neal Shover, "Burglary," in Michael Tonry, ed., *Crime and Justice: A Review of Research* (73–113) (Chicago: University of Chicago Press, 1991), 103; Walters, *Criminal Lifestyle*, 145.

28. Marcus Felson, "Routine Activities and Crime Prevention in the Developing Metropolis," *Criminology* 25 (1987): 911–31.

CHAPTER 7

1. Mieczkowski, "Crack Dealing on the Street," 155.

2. See Johnson et al., "Emerging Models of Crack Distribution"; Maher and Daly, "Women in the Street-Level Drug Economy," 471; Mieczkowski, "'Geeking Up' and Throwing Down"; see also Georg Simmel, *The Sociology of Georg Simmel*, ed. Kurt Wolff (New York: Free Press, 1950).

3. Mieczkowski, "Crack Dealing on the Street," 155.

4. Mieczkowski, "Crack Dealing on the Street," 157.

5. Adler, *Wheeling and Dealing*, 80.

6. See Elijah Anderson, *The Code of the Streets* (Chicago: University of Chicago Press, in press); Bourgois, *In Search of Respect*; Sanchez-Jankowski, *Islands in the Street*; Shover, *Great Pretenders*; Walter B. Miller, "Lower-Class Culture as a Generating Milieu of Gang Delinquency," *Journal of Social Issues* 14 (1958): 5–19; Terry Williams, *The Cocaine Kids* (Reading, Mass.: Addison-Wesley, 1989).

7. Reuter et al., *Money from Crime*, viii.

8. Gary S. Becker, *The Economic Approach to Human Behavior* (Chicago: University of Chicago Press, 1976), 8.

9. Cf. Adler, *Wheeling and Dealing*.

10. Carol A. Heimer, "Social Structure, Psychology, and the Estimation of Risk," *Annual Review of Sociology* 14 (1988): 510.

11. See Bourgois, *In Search of Respect*, 35; Elliot Liebow, *Tally's Corner* (Boston: Little, Brown, 1967).

12. Michael Gottfredson and Travis Hirschi, "The True Value of Lambda Would Appear to Be Zero: An Essay on Career Criminals, Criminal Careers, Selective Incapacitation, Cohort Studies, and Related Topics," *Criminology* 24 (1986): 213–34.

13. A. D. Chandler, *Strategy and Structure: Chapters in the History of the Industrial Enterprise* (Cambridge: MIT Press, 1962).

14. Chris Stetkiewitz, "Surging U.S. Payrolls Show Economy Remains Robust," Reuters News Service, from Yahoo! Search Engine, February 6, 1998; United States Department of Labor, *Quarterly Report* (Washington, D.C.: U.S. Government Printing Office, 1998).

15. See Fagan, "Drug Selling and Licit Income"; Richard B. Freeman, "Why Do So Many Young American Men Commit Crimes and What Might We Do about It?" (National Bureau of Economic Research, Working Paper Series, 1996), 14, 16; John M. Hagedorn, *People and Folks* (Chicago: Lake View Press, 1988); Reuter et al., *Money from Crime*.

16. See James Coleman, *Foundations of Social Theory* (Cambridge: Harvard University Press, 1990); Robert J. Sampson and John Laub, *Crime in the Making* (Cambridge: Harvard University Press, 1993).

17. Bill McCarthy and John Hagan, "Getting into Street Crime: The Structure and Process of Criminal Embeddedness," *Social Science Research* 24 (1995): 87; see also Coleman, *Foundations*.

18. William Form, "On the Degradation of Skills," *Annual Review of Sociology* 13 (1987): 29–47.

19. Bourgois, *In Search of Respect*; Shover, *Great Pretenders*.

20. Ken Auletta, *The Underclass* (New York: Vintage, 1982), 200.

21. See Andrew Golub and Bruce D. Johnson, "Monitoring the Decline in the Crack Epidemic with Data from the Drug Use Forecasting Program," Final Report to National Institute of Justice (New York: John Jay College of Criminal Justice, 1997).

22. Anthony Collings, "Meth Abuse Spreads, with Violent Results," CNN Interactive, from Yahoo! Search Engine, February 13, 1996.

23. Cesar, "Younger Arrestees."

24. On the number of heroin users, see Office of National Drug Control Policy, "Pulse Check"; W. Rhodes, P. Scheiman, and K. Carlson, "What America's Users Spend on Illegal Drugs, 1988–1991" (Washington, D.C.: Abt Associates, 1993); and Christopher S. Wren, "U.S. Convenes Drug Experts to Grapple with Rise in Heroin Use," *New York Times*, September 30, 1997, A17; on use patterns, see National Center on Addiction and Substance Abuse, press release, August 13, 1997; on emergency room visits, see National Institutes of Health, "Effective Medical Treatment of Heroin Addiction," Online Bulletin, 1997; and Drug Abuse Warning Network (DAWN), "Preliminary Estimates of Drug-Related Emergency Department Episodes," Report number 14 (Washington, D.C.: U.S. Department of Health and Human Services, 1996).

25. On heroin purity, see National Narcotics Intelligence Consumers Committee, *The NNICC Report 1995: The Supply of Illicit Drugs to the United States* (Washington, D.C.: U.S. Government Printing Office, 1996); United Press International, "Heroin Suspected in Teen Death," from Yahoo! Search Engine, April 19, 1997; on seizures from South America, see Drug Enforcement Administration (DEA), "The 1995 Heroin Signature Program," *Intelligence Bulletin* (1996); on snortable heroin, see Johnson et al., "Natural Transitions"; United Press International, "Forty-five Drug Arrests Made in Texas," from Yahoo! Search Engine, December 5, 1997; United Press International, "Heroin Use on the Rise Nationwide," from Yahoo! Search Engine, July 22, 1997.

26. On snorting to injection, see Geoffrey Pearson, *The New Heroin Users* (New York: Basic Blackwell, 1987); on invincibility, see Walters, *Criminal Lifestyle*; on protease inhibitors, see United Press International, "AIDS Treatments Add to Risky Behavior," from Yahoo! Search Engine, August 13, 1997; on factors related to drug market stability, see Goldstein, "The Drugs / Violence Nexus"; Alisse Waterson, *Street Addiction: The Political Economy* (Philadelphia: Temple University Press, 1993).

27. On crack's decline, see Eric Baumer, Janet Lauritsen, Richard Rosenfeld, and Richard Wright, "The Influence of Crack Cocaine on Robbery, Burglary, and Homicide Rates: A Cross-City Longitudinal Analysis," *Journal of Research in Crime and Delinquency* 35 (1998): 316–40; Alfred Blumstein, "Youth Violence, Guns, and the Illicit Drug Industry," *Journal of Criminal Law and Criminology* 86 (1995): 10–36; Blumstein and Rosenfeld, "Explaining Recent Trends"; on drugs and crime, see David N. Nurco, Ira H. Cisin, and Mitchell Balter, "Addict Careers: Trends across Time," *International Journal of the Addictions* 16 (1981): 1327–72; John W. Shaffer, David Nurco, John C. Ball, and Timothy W. Kinlock, "The Frequency of Nonnarcotic Drug Use and Its Relationship to Criminal Activity among Narcotics

Addicts," *Comprehensive Psychiatry* 26 (1985): 558–66; on crack and crime, revenge, antagonism, etc., see Inciardi et al., *Street Kids*.

28. Baumer et al., "The Influence of Crack Cocaine," 22.

29. On the economics of crack's decline, see Baumer et al., "The Influence of Crack Cocaine"; on the growth of the cashless society, see Marcus Felson, "A 'Routine Activity' Analysis of Recent Crime Reductions," *Criminologist* 22 (1997): 3; Wright and Decker, *Armed Robbers*; United States Census Bureau, *Statistical Abstract of the United States, 1996* (Washington, D.C.: U.S. Government Printing Office, 1996), Table 793; on sex-for-crack, see Inciardi, "Kingrats"; on drugs as the new street currency, see Fleisher, *Beggars and Thieves*.

30. Cesar, "Younger Arrestees"; Drug Use Forecasting (DUF), *Annual Report*; see also Golub and Johnson, "Crack's Decline."

31. Terry Furst, "The Stigmatized Image of the Crackhead," unpublished manuscript (New York: National Drug Research Institute, 1995), 12.

32. See, e.g., Sampson and Laub, *Crime in the Making*.

33. James F. Short Jr. and Fred L. Strodtbeck, *Group Process and Gang Delinquency* (Chicago: University of Chicago Press, 1965), 242.

34. Michael Tonry, *Malign Neglect* (New York: Oxford University Press, 1995).

35. James O. Finckenaur, *Scared Straight! and the Panacea Phenomenon* (Englewood Cliffs, N.J.: Prentice-Hall, 1982); I. L. Janis and S. Feshback, "Effects of Fear-Arousing Communications," *Journal of Abnormal and Social Psychology* 48 (1953): 78–92; G. F. Vito, "Developments in Shock Probation: A Review of Research Findings and Policy Implications," *Federal Probation* 48 (1984): 21–34.

SELECTED BIBLIOGRAPHY

Adler, Patricia A. *Wheeling and Dealing*. New York: Columbia University Press, 1985.

Agar, Michael. *Ripping and Running: A Formal Ethnography of Urban Heroin Addicts*. New York: Seminar Press, 1973.

Anderson, Elijah. *The Code of the Streets*. Chicago: University of Chicago Press, in press.

Anderson, Elijah. *Streetwise*. Chicago: University of Chicago Press, 1990.

Baumer, Eric, Janet Lauritsen, Richard Rosenfeld, and Richard Wright. "The Influence of Crack Cocaine on Robbery, Burglary, and Homicide Rates: A Cross-City Longitudinal Analysis." *Journal of Research in Crime and Delinquency* 35 (1998): 316–40.

Blumstein, Alfred. "Youth Violence, Guns, and the Illicit Drug Industry." *Journal of Criminal Law and Criminology* 86 (1995): 10–36.

Blumstein, Alfred, and Richard Rosenfeld. "Explaining Recent Trends in U.S. Homicide Rates." *Journal of Criminology and Criminal Law* (1998).

Bourgois, Philippe. *In Search of Respect: Selling Crack in El Barrio*. Cambridge: Cambridge University Press, 1995.

Bourgois, Philippe, and Eloise Dunlap. "Exorcising Sex-for-Crack in Harlem: An Ethnographic Perspective from Harlem." In Mitchell S. Ratner, ed., *Crack Pipe as Pimp: An Ethnographic*

Investigation of Sex-for-Crack Exchanges. New York: Lexington, 1993.

Cesar. "Younger Arrestees in U.S. Favor Marijuana, Older Arrestees Stay with Cocaine." *Cesar Fax*, vol. 6, issue 26, July 7 (1997).

Cesar. "Marijuana Replacing Cocaine as Drug of Choice among Adult Arrestees." *Cesar Fax*, vol. 6, issue 25, June 30 (1997).

Chitwood, Dale D., James E. Rivers, and James A. Inciardi. *The American Pipe Dream: Crack Cocaine and the Inner City*. New York: Harcourt Brace, 1996.

Decker, Scott H., and Barrik Van Winkle. *Life in the Gang*. Cambridge: Cambridge University Press, 1996.

Drug Abuse Warning Network (DAWN). "Preliminary Estimates of Drug-Related Emergency Department Episodes." Report number 14. Washington, D.C.: U.S. Department of Health and Human Services, 1996.

Drug Enforcement Administration (DEA). "The 1995 Heroin Signature Program." *Intelligence Bulletin* (1996).

Drug Enforcement Administration (DEA). "The Supply of Illicit Drugs to the United States." Washington, D.C.: National Narcotics Intelligence Consumers Committee, 1995.

Drug Use Forecasting (DUF). *Quarterly Report*. Washington, D.C.: National Institute of Justice, 1997.

Drug Use Forecasting (DUF). *Annual Report*. Washington, D.C.: National Institute of Justice, 1996.

Dunlap, Eloise, and Bruce D. Johnson. "The Setting for the Crack Era: Macro Forces, Micro Consequences." *Journal of Psychoactive Drugs* 24 (1992): 307–21.

Durkheim, Emile. *The Division of Labor in Society*. New York: Free Press, 1964.

Fagan, Jeffrey. "Drug Selling and Licit Income in Distressed Neighborhoods: The Economic Lives of Street-Level Drug Users and Dealers." In Adele V. Harrell and George E. Peterson, eds., *Drugs, Crime, and Social Isolation* (99–146). Washington, D.C.: Urban Institute Press, 1991.

Fagan, Jeffrey, and Ko-lin Chin. "Initiation into Crack and Cocaine: A Tale of Two Epidemics." *Contemporary Drug Problems* 16 (1989): 579–618.

Ferrell, Jeff. "Criminological Verstehen: Inside the Immediacy of Crime." In Jeff Ferrell and Mark S. Hamm, eds., *Ethnography at the Edge: Crime, Deviance, and Field Research*. Boston: Northeastern University Press, 1998.

Fleisher, Mark S. *Beggars and Thieves*. Madison: University of Wisconsin Press, 1995.

Furst, Terry. "The Stigmatized Image of the Crackhead." Unpublished manuscript, National Drug Research Institute, New York, 1995.

Glassner, Barry, and Cheryl Carpenter. "The Feasibility of an Ethnographic Study of Property Offenders: A Report Prepared for the National Institute of Justice." Washington, D.C.: National Institute of Justice, 1985.

Goldstein, Paul J. "The Drugs / Violence Nexus: A Tripartite Conceptual Framework." *Journal of Drug Issues* 15 (1985): 493–506.

Golub, Andrew, and Bruce D. Johnson. "Crack's Decline: Some Surprises across U.S. Cities." *Research in Brief* (p. 11). Washington, D.C.: National Institute of Justice, 1997.

Golub, Andrew, and Bruce D. Johnson. "Monitoring the Decline in the Crack Epidemic with Data from the Drug Use Forecasting Program." Final Report to National Institute of Justice. New York: John Jay College of Criminal Justice, 1997.

Hagan, John, and Bill McCarthy. *Mean Streets: Youth Crime and Homelessness*. New York: Cambridge University Press, 1997.

Hamid, Ansley. "The Developmental Cycle of a Drug Epidemic: The Cocaine Smoking Epidemic of 1981–1991." *Journal of Psychoactive Drugs* 24 (1992): 337–48.

Humphreys, Laud. *Tearoom Trade*. New York: de Gruyter, 1970.

Inciardi, James A. "Kingrats, Chicken Heads, Slow Necks, Freaks, and Blood Suckers: A Glimpse at the Miami Sex-for-Crack Market." In Mitchell S. Ratner, ed., *Crack Pipe as Pimp*. New York: Lexington Books, 1993.

Inciardi, James A., Ruth Horowitz, and Anne E. Pottieger. *Street Kids, Street Drugs, Street Crime*. Belmont, Calif.: Wadsworth, 1993.

Inciardi, James A., D. Lockwood, and Annie E. Pottieger. *Women and Crack Cocaine*. New York: Macmillan, 1993.

Jacobs, Bruce A. "Contingent Ties: Undercover Drug Officers' Use of Informants." *British Journal of Sociology* 48 (1997): 35–53.

Jacobs, Bruce A. "Anticipatory Undercover Operations in High Schools." *Journal of Criminal Justice* 22 (1994): 445–57.

Jacobs, Bruce A. "Undercover Deception Clues: A Case of Restrictive Deterrence." *Criminology* 31 (1993): 281–99.

Johnson, Bruce D. "The Crack Era in New York City." *Addiction and Recovery* (May-June 1991): 24–27.

Johnson, Bruce D., Eloise Dunlap, Kathleen Boyle, and Bruce Jacobs. "Natural Transitions in Crack Distribution/Abuse." For National Institute on Drug Abuse. New York: National Drug Research Institute, 1997.

Johnson, Bruce D., George Thomas, and Andrew Golub. "Heroin Use among Manhattan Arrestees from the Heroin and Crack Eras." In James A. Inciardi, ed., *Heroin in the Age of Crack Cocaine*. Beverly Hills: Sage, 1997.

Johnson, Bruce D., Andrew Golub, and Jeffrey Fagan. "Careers in Crack, Drug Use, Drug Distribution, and Nondrug Criminality." *Crime and Delinquency* 41 (1995): 275–95.

Johnson, Bruce D., and Mangai Natarajan. "Strategies to Avoid Arrest: Crack Sellers' Response to Intensified Policing." *American Journal of Police* 14 (1995): 49–69.

Johnson, Bruce D., Mangai Nataranjan, Eloise Dunlap, and Elsayed Elmoghazy. "Crack Abusers and Noncrack Abusers: Profiles of Drug Use, Drug Sales, and Nondrug Criminality." *Journal of Drug Issues* 24 (1994): 117–41.

Johnson, Bruce D., Ansley Hamid, and Harry Sanabria. "Emerging Models of Crack Distribution." In Thomas Mieczkowski, ed., *Drugs and Crime: A Reader* (56–78). Boston: Allyn and Bacon, 1992.

Johnson, Bruce D., Terry Williams, Kojo A. Dei, and Harry Sanabria. "Drug Abuse in the Inner City: Impact on Hard Drug Users and the Community." In Michael Tonry and James Q. Wilson, eds., *Drugs and Crime*. Chicago: University of Chicago Press, 1990.

Klein, Malcolm. *The American Street Gang*. Oxford: Oxford University Press, 1995.

Lauritsen, Janet L., Robert J. Sampson, and John H. Laub. "The

Link between Offending and Victimization among Adolescents." *Criminology* 29 (1991): 265–91.

McCarthy, Bill, and John Hagan. "Getting into Street Crime: The Structure and Process of Criminal Embeddedness." *Social Science Research* 24 (1995): 63–95.

MacCoun, Robert, and Peter Reuter. "Are the Wages of Sin $30 an Hour? Economic Aspects of Street-Level Drug Dealing." *Crime and Delinquency* 38 (1992): 477–91.

Maher, Lisa, and Kathleen Daly. "Women in the Street-Level Drug Economy: Continuity or Change?" *Criminology* 34 (1996): 465–91.

Manning, Peter K. *The Narcs' Game*. Cambridge: MIT Press, 1980.

Mieczkowski, Thomas. "Crack Dealing on the Street: The Crew System and the Crack House." *Justice Quarterly* 9 (1992): 151–63.

Mieczkowski, Thomas. "Some Observations on the Scope of Crack Use and Distribution." In Thomas Mieczkowski, ed., *Drugs and Crime: A Reader* (32–55). Boston: Allyn and Bacon, 1992.

Mieczkowski, Thomas. "Crack Distribution in Detroit." *Contemporary Drug Problems* 17 (1990).

Mieczkowski, Thomas. "'Geeking Up' and Throwing Down: Heroin Street Life in Detroit." *Criminology* 24 (1986): 645–66.

Office of National Drug Control Policy. "Pulse Check: National Trends in Drug Abuse." Washington, D.C., 1996.

Office of National Drug Control Policy. *Drugs and Crime Data*. Washington, D.C.: U.S. Government Printing Office, 1996.

Padilla, Felix M. *The Gang as an American Enterprise*. New Brunswick: Rutgers University Press, 1992.

Polsky, Ned. *Hustlers, Beats, and Others*. Chicago: Aldine, 1967.

Prus, Robert. "Purchasing Products for Resale: Assessing Suppliers as 'Partners-in-Trade'." *Symbolic Interaction* 7 (1984): 249–78.

Reuter, Peter, Robert MacCoun, and Patrick Murphy. *Money from Crime*. Santa Monica: Rand, 1990.

Riley, Jack K. "Homicide and Drugs: A Tale of Six Cities." *Homicide Studies* 2 (1998): 176–205.

Riley, Jack K. *Crack, Powder, and Heroin: Drug Use and Purchase Patterns in Six U.S. Cities*. Washington, D.C.: National Institute of Justice and The Office of the National Drug Control Policy, 1997.

Rosenfeld, Richard, and Scott H. Decker. "Consent to Search and Seize: Evaluating an Innovative Youth Firearms Suppression Program." *Law and Contemporary Problems* 59 (1996): 197–219.

Rosenfeld, Richard. "The St. Louis Homicide Project: Local Responses to a National Problem." Unpublished manuscript, 1991.

Sampson, Robert J., and John Laub. *Crime in the Making*. Cambridge: Harvard University Press, 1993.

Sanchez-Jankowski, Martin. *Islands in the Street*. Berkeley: University of California Press, 1991.

Short, James F., Jr., *Poverty, Ethnicity, and Violent Crime*. Boulder: Westview, 1997.

Short, James F., Jr., and Fred L. Strodtbeck. *Group Process and Gang Delinquency*. Chicago: University of Chicago Press, 1965.

Shover, Neal. *Great Pretenders*. Boulder: Westview, 1996.

Skolnick, Jerome H., Theodore Correl, Elizabeth Navarro, and Roger Rabb. "The Social Structure of Street Drug Dealing." In Larry K. Gaines and Peter B. Kraska, eds., *Drugs, Crime, and Justice* (159–91). Prospect Heights, Ill.: Waveland Press, 1997.

Waldorf, Dan. "Don't Be Your Own Best Customer: Drug Use of San Francisco Gang Drug Sellers." *Crime, Law, and Social Change* 19 (1993): 1–15.

Waldorf, Dan. *Careers in Dope*. Englewood Cliffs, N.J.: Prentice-Hall, 1973.

Walters, Glenn B. *The Criminal Lifestyle*. Newbury Park, Calif.: Sage, 1990.

Williams, Terry. *Crackhouse*. Reading, Mass.: Addison-Wesley, 1992.

Williams, Terry. *The Cocaine Kids*. Reading, Mass.: Addison-Wesley, 1989.

Williams, Terry, Eloise Dunlap, Bruce D. Johnson, and Ansley Hamid. "Personal Safety in Dangerous Places." *Journal of Contemporary Ethnography* 21 (1992): 343–74.

Wilson, William Julius. *When Work Disappears*. New York: Knopf, 1996.

Wilson, William Julius. *The Truly Disadvantaged*. Chicago: University of Chicago Press, 1987.

Wright, Richard T., and Scott H. Decker. *Armed Robbers in Action*. Boston: Northeastern University Press, 1997.

Wright, Richard T., and Scott H. Decker. *Burglars on the Job*. Boston: Northeastern University Press, 1994.

Wright, Richard T., and Michael Stein. "Seeing Ourselves: Exploring the Social Production of Criminological Knowledge in a Qualitative Methods Course." *Journal of Criminal Justice Education* 7 (1996): 66–77.

INDEX

police (*see also* undercover police):
bearing and gait, 107; deception
of, 89–90; effect on market, 63–
64; perceptual shorthands, 18;
researcher pullovers, 15–19; researcher ride-alongs, 24
posturing, 80–81
potential customers, 116
poverty, 9, 26
predation, 66, 119
presale testing, 74
press reporting, 3
pricing, 46
primos, 5–6, 48
profitability, 4–5, 46, 48
prostitution, 36
protected markets, 62–63
pseudofriendships, 60–61
psychedelic drugs, 124
public transfer payments, 47
punishment, certainty *vs.* severity,
85

quoted material, use of, 25

race, of respondents, 21
repeat violent offenders, 17
reputation, 31, 75, 80–81
research methodology, 7
researcher: appearance, 14–15;
credibility, 16–19; police
pullovers, 15–19; police ride-
alongs, 24; robbery of, 39
respect, 27, 29, 45, 119
respondents: anonymity of, 22, 25;
characteristics, 19–23; helpful-
ness, 25; screening, 22–23
restrictive deterrence, 115–16
retribution, 80–81
revenge, 76
revenue: and respect, 29; urgency to
increase, 103
ripoffs, 66
risk, fewer transactions for larger
amounts, 47
robbery: in cash-rich economies,
127; of dealers, 76–79, 80; of
"high-catting" persons, 31; as
occupation, 41

safety, with multiple dealers, 78,
95–96, 97–98
St. Louis: conditions favoring study,
8–9; police ride-alongs, 24; police vehicles in bad weather, 97;
south city, 56; strip search prohibitions, 88
sales: taking turns, 53; time of day,
53–54; time of month, 47
sanctions, deterrent power of,
85
scams, 69–73, 74–76
scanning, 104–5
SCAT (street-corner apprehension
team), 13–14
self-indulgence, 41
self-reliance, 44–45, 119
sellers. *See* dealers
setting, 8–11
sexual behavior, high risk, 125
shared social history, 74
shortchanging, 74
sleight of hand, 90–91
smack. *See* heroin
small packages, 46–47
snowball samples, 19–20
social capital accumulation, 123
social skills, 28
social systems, 7
society, isolation from, 116
solicitational argot, 109–11
spending, 29–32
stagnating markets, 81–82, 84, 102,
117, 122
staring, implications of, 104–5
stash stealing, 83–84, 121
stashing, 83–84, 86–87
stems, 106
stigma of use, 5–6, 38
straight shooters, 106
street conduct norms, 28, 104
street exchanges, 73–76
street gangs, 9, 10
street selling, 49–56
strip searches, 88
studies, 7
study population, 10–11
supply: frequency of purchase, 47;
seller access to, 44